All For Love: And The Pilgrim To Compostella

Robert Southey

S.H. 1829

ALL FOR LOVE;

8/

AND

THE PILGRIM TO COMPOSTELLA.

BY

ROBERT SOUTHEY,

POET LAUREATE, &

LONDON:

JOHN MURRAY, ALBEMARLE STREET.

MDCCCXXIX.

324.

TO

CAROLINE BOWLES.

Could I look forward to a distant day
With hope of building some elaborate lay,
Then would I wait till worthier strains of mine
Might bear inscribed thy name, O Caroline!
For I would, while my voice is heard on earth,
Bear witness to thy genius and thy worth.
But we have both been taught to feel with fear
How frail the tenure of existence here,
What unforeseen calamities prevent,
Alas, how oft! the best resolved intent;
And therefore this poor volume I address
To thee, dear friend, and sister Poetess.

ROBERT SOUTHEY.

KESWICK, 21 FEB. 1829.

CONTENTS.

ALL FOR LOVE,

OR

A SINNER WELL SAVED.

B

THE story of the following Poem is taken from a Life of St. Basil, ascribed to his contemporary St. Amphilochius, Bishop of Iconium; a Latin version of which, made by Cardinal Ursus in the ninth century, is inserted by Rosweyde, among the Lives of the Fathers, in his compilation *Historiæ Eremiticæ*. The original had not then been printed, but Rosweyde obtained a copy of it from the Royal Library at Paris. He intimates no suspicion concerning the authenticity of the life, or the truth of this particular legend; observing only, that *hæc narratio apud solum invenitur Amphilochium*. It is, indeed, the flower of the work, and as such had been culled by some earlier translator than Ursus.

The very learned Dominican, P. François Combefis, published the original with a version of his own, and endeavoured to establish its authenticity in opposition to Baronius, who supposed the life to have been written by some other Amphilochius, not by the Bishop of Iconium. Had Combefis possessed powers of mind equal to his erudition, he might even then have been in some degree prejudiced upon this subject, for, according to Baillet, *il avoit un attachement particulier pour S. Basile*. His version is inserted in the *Acta Sanctorum* (Jun. t. ii. pp. 937—957). But the Bollandist Baert brands the life there as apocryphal; and in his annotations treats Combefis more rudely, it may be suspected, than he would have done, had he not belonged to a rival and hostile order.

Should the reader be desirous of comparing the Poem with the Legend, he may find the story, as transcribed from Rosweyde, among the Notes.

B 2

ALL FOR LOVE,

OR

A SINNER WELL SAVED.

I.

A Youth hath entered the Sorcerer's door,
    But he dares not lift his eye,
For his knees fail and his flesh quakes,
    And his heart beats audibly.

" Look up, young man!" the Sorcerer said,
    " Lay open thy wishes to me!
Or art thou too modest to tell thy tale?
    If so,.. I can tell it thee.

" Thy name is Eleëmon;
Proterius's freedman thou art;
And on Cyra, thy Master's daughter,
Thou hast madly fix'd thy heart.

" But fearing (as thou well mayest fear!)
The high-born Maid to woo,
Thou hast tried what secret prayers and vows
And sacrifice might do.

" Thou hast prayed unto all Saints in Heaven,
And to Mary their vaunted Queen;
And little furtherance hast thou found
From them, or from her, I ween!

" And thou, I know, the Ancient Gods,
In hope forlorn hast tried,
If haply Venus might obtain
The maiden for thy bride.

" On Jove and Phœbus thou hast call'd,
    And on Astarte's name;
And on her, who still at Ephesus
    Retains a faded fame.

" Thy voice to Baal hath been raised;
    To Nile's old Deities;
And to all Gods of elder time
Adored by men in every clime
When they ruled earth, seas and skies.

" Their Images are deaf!
    Their Oracles are dumb!
And therefore thou, in thy despair,
    To Abibas art come.

" Aye, because neither Saints nor Gods
    Thy pleasure will fulfil,
Thou comest to me, Eleëmon,
    To ask if Satan will!

" I answer thee, Yes.   But a faint heart
Can never accomplish its ends !
Put thy trust boldly in him, and be sure
He never forsakes his friends."

While Eleëmon listened
He shuddered inwardly,
At the ugly voice of Abibas,
And the look in his wicked eye.

And he could then almost have given
His fatal purpose o'er ;
But his Good Angel had left him
When he entered the Sorcerer's door.

So in the strength of evil shame,
His mind the young man knit
Into a desperate resolve,
For his bad purpose fit.

" Let thy Master give me what I seek,
O Servant of Satan," he said,
" As I ask firmly, and for his
Renounce all other aid!

" Time presses.   Cyra is content
To bid the world farewell,
And pass her days, a virgin vowed,
Among Emmelia's sisterhood,
The tenant of a cell.

" Thus hath her Father will'd, that so
A life of rigour here below
May fit her for the skies;
And Heaven acceptably receive
His costliest sacrifice.

" The admiring people say of this
That Angels, or that Saints in bliss,

The holy thought inspire;
And she is called a blessed Maid,
And he a happy Sire.

" Through Cappadocia far and wide
The news hath found its way,
And crowds to Cæsarea flock
To attend the solemn day.

" The robes are ready, rich with gold,
Even like a bridal dress,
Which at the altar she will wear
When self-devoted she stands there
In all her loveliness.

" And that coarse habit too, which she
Must then put on, is made,
Therein to be for life and death
Unchangeably array'd.

" This night,.. this precious night is ours,..
    Late, late, I come to you;
But all that must be dared, or done,
    Prepared to dare and do."

" Thou hast hesitated long !" said Abibas,
    " And thou hast done amiss,
In praying to Him whom I name not,
    That it never might come to this!

" But thou hast chosen thy part, and here thou art;
    And thou shalt have thy desire.
    And tho' at the eleventh hour
Thou hast come to serve our Prince of Power,
    He will give thee in full thine hire.

" These Tablets take; (he wrote as he spake,)
    " My letters, which thou art to bear,
    Wherein I shall commend thee
To the Prince of the Powers of the Air.

" Go from the North Gate out, and take
On a Pagan's Tomb thy stand;
And, looking to the North, hold up
The Tablets in thy hand :

" And call the Spirits of the Air,
That they my messenger may bear
To the place whither he would pass,
And there present him to their Prince
In the name of Abibas.

" The passage will be swift and safe,
No danger awaits thee beyond;
Thou wilt only have now to sign and seal,
And hereafter to pay the Bond."

II.

SHUNNING human sight, like a thief in the night,
    Eleëmon made no delay,
      But went unto a Pagan's tomb
      Beside the public way.

    Inclosed with barren elms it stood,
      There planted when the dead
      Within the last abode of man
      Had been deposited.

    And thrice ten years those barren trees,
      Enjoying light and air,
  Had grown and flourished, while the dead
      In darkness mouldered there.

Long had they overtopt the tomb :
And closed was now that upper room
Where friends were wont to pour,
Upon the honoured dust below,
Libations thro' the floor.

There on that unblest monument
The young man took his stand,
And northward he the tablets held
In his uplifted hand.

A courage not his own he felt,
A wicked fortitude,
Wherewith bad Influences unseen
That hour his heart endued.

The rising Moon grew pale in heaven
At that unhappy sight;
And all the blessed Stars seem'd then

To close their twinkling light;
And a shuddering in the elms was heard,
Tho' winds were still that night.

He call'd the Spirits of the Air,
He call'd them in the name
Of Abibas; and at the call
The attendant Spirits came.

A strong hand which he could not see
Took his uplifted hand;
He felt a strong arm circle him,
And lift him from his stand;

A whirr of unseen wings he heard
About him everywhere,
Which onward, with a mighty force,
Impell'd him thro' the air.

Fast thro' the middle sky and far
 It hurried him along;
The Hurrican is not so swift,
 The Torrent not so strong:

The Lightning travels not so fast,
 The Sunbeams not so far:
And now behind him he hath left
 The Moon and every Star.

And still erect as on the tomb
 In impious act he stood,
Is he rapt onward ... onward ... still
 In that fix'd attitude.

But as he from the living world
 Approach'd where Spirits dwell,
His bearers there in thinner air
 Were dimly visible;

Shapeless, and scarce to be descried
   In darkness where they flew;
But still as they advanced, the more
   And more distinct they grew:

And when their way fast-speeding they
   Thro' their own region went,
Then were they in their substance seen,
The angelic form, the fiendish mien,
   Face, look and lineament.

Behold where dawns before them now,
   Far off, the boreal ray,
Sole daylight of that frozen zone,
   The limit of their way.

In that drear realm of outer night,
Like the shadow, or the ghost of light,
   It moved in the restless skies,

c

And went and came, like a feeble flame
That flickers before it dies.

There the Fallen Seraph reign'd supreme
Amid the utter waste;
There on the everlasting ice
His dolorous throne was placed.

Son of the Morning! is it then
For this that thou hast given
Thy seat, pre-eminent among
The hierarchies of Heaven?

As if dominion here could joy
To blasted pride impart;
Or this cold region slake the fire
Of Hell within the heart!

Thither the Evil Angels bear

The youth, and rendering homage there
.Their service they evince,
And in the name of Abibas
Present him to their Prince:

Just as they seized him when he made
The Sorcerer's mandate known,
.In that same act and attitude
·They set him before the throne.

The Fallen Seraph cast on him
A dark disdainful, look;
And from his raised hand scornfully
The proffered tablets took.

" Aye,.. love!" he cried. " It serves me well.
· There was the Trojan boy,,.
His love brought forth a ten years' war,
And ·fired the towers of Troy.

" And when my own Mark Antony
  Against young Cæsar strove,
And Rome's whole world was set in arms,
  The cause was,.. all for love!

" Some for ambition sell themselves,
  By avarice some are driven;
Pride, envy, hatred, best will move
Some souls, and some for only love
Renounce their hopes of Heaven.

" Yes, of all human follies, love,
  Methinks, hath served me best.
The Apple had done but little for me
  If Eve had not done the rest.

" Well then, young Amorist, whom love
  Hath brought unto this pass,
I am willing to perform the word
  Of my servant Abibas.

" Thy Master's daughter shall be thine,
　　And with her sire's consent;
　And not more to thy heart's desire
　　Than to her own content.

" Yea, more,.. I give thee with the girl,
　　Thine after-days to bless,
Health, wealth, long life, and whatsoe'er
　　The world calls happiness.

" But, mark me!.. on conditions, youth!
　　No paltering here we know!
　Dost thou here, solemnly, this hour
　　Thy hope of Heaven forego?

　Dost thou renounce thy baptism,
　　And bind thyself to me,
　My woeful portion to partake
　　Thro' all eternity?

" No lurking purpose shall avail,
When youth may fail and courage quail,
    To cheat me by contrition!
I will have thee written down among
    The Children of Perdition.

" Remember, I deceive thee not,
    Nor have I tempted thee!
Thou comest of thine own accord,
    And actest knowingly.

" Dost thou, who now to choose art free,
    For ever pledge thyself to me?
As I shall help thee, say!"...
    " I do; so help me, Satan!" said
    The wilful castaway.

" A resolute answer:" quoth the Fiend;
    " And now then, Child of Dust,

In farther proof of that firm heart,
Thou wilt sign a Bond before we part,
For I take thee not on trust!"

Swift as thought a scroll and a reed were brought,
And to Eleëmon's breast,
Just where the heart-stroke plays, the point
Of the reed was gently prest.

It pierced not in, nor touch'd the skin;
But the sense that it caused was such,
As when an electric pellet of light
Comes forcibly out at a touch.

A sense no sooner felt than gone.
But with that short feeling then
A drop of his heart's-blood came forth
And fill'd the fatal pen.

And with that pen accurst, he sign'd
The execrable scroll,
Whereby he to perdition bound
His miserable soul.

" Eleëmon, Eleëmon!" then said the Demon,
" The girl shall be thine,
By the tie she holds divine,
Till time that tie shall sever;
And by this writing thou art mine,
For ever and ever and ever!"

III.

Look at yon silent dwelling now!
  A heavenly sight is there,
Where Cyra in her chamber kneels
  Before the Cross in prayer.

She is not loth to leave the world;
  For she hath been taught with joy
To think that prayer and praise thenceforth
  Will be her life's employ.

And thus her mind hath she inclined,
  Her pleasure being still,
(An only child and motherless,)
  To do her Father's will.

The moonlight falls upon her face,
    Upraised in fervour meek,
While peaceful tears of piety
    Are stealing down her cheek.

That duty done, the harmless maid
    Disposed herself to rest;
No sin, no sorrow in her soul,
    No trouble in her breast.

But when upon the pillow then,
    Composed, she laid her head,
She little thought what unseen Powers
    Kept watch beside her bed.

A double ward had she that night,
    When evil near her drew;
Her own Good Angel guarding her,
    And Eleëmon's too.

Their charge it was to keep her safe
  From all unholy things;
And o'er her while she slept, they spread
  The shadow of their wings.

So when an Evil Dream drew nigh
  They barr'd him from access,
Nor suffered him to reach her with
  A breath of sinfulness.

But with his instigations they
  A hallowing influence blent,
And made his fiendish ministry
  Subserve to their intent.

Thus while in troubled sleep she lay,
  Strange impulses were given,
Emotions earthly and of earth,
  With heavenly ones of Heaven,

And now the nightingale hath ceased
Her strain, who all night long
Hath in the garden rosier trill'd
A rich and rapturous song.

The storks on roof and dome and tower
Forbear their clattering din,
As now the motions and the sounds
Of daily life begin.

Then as from dreams that seem'd no dreams
The wondering Maid awoke,
A low sweet voice was in her ear;
Such as we might expect to hear
If some Good Angel spoke.

According with her dreams, it said,
" So, Cyra, must it be ;
The duties of a wedded life
Hath Heaven ordain'd for thee."

This was no dream full well she knew;
    For open-eyed she lay,
Conscious of thought and wakefulness
    And in the light of day;
And twice it spake, if doubt had been,
    To do all doubt away.

Alas! but how shall she make known
    This late and sudden change?
    Or how obtain belief for what
    Even to herself is strange?

How will her Father brook a turn
    That must to all seem shame?
How bear to think that vulgar tongues
    Are busy with her name!

That she should for a voice,.. a dream,..
    Expose herself to be the theme
    Of wonder and of scorn;..

Public as her intent had been,
And this the appointed morn!

The Nuns even now are all alert;
The altar hath been drest,
The scissars that should clip her hair
Provided, and the black hood there,
And there the sable vest.

And there the Priests are robing now;
The Singers in their station;
Hark! in the city she can hear
The stir of expectation!

Thro' every gate the people pour,
And guests on roof and porch and tower
Expectant take their place;
The streets are swarming, and the church
Already fills apace.

Speak, then, she must: her heart she felt
    This night had changed its choice;
  Nor dared the Maiden disobey,..
  Nor did she wish to, (sooth to say),..
    That sweet and welcome voice.

  Her Father comes: she studies not
    For gloss, or for pretence;
The plain straight course will Cyra take,
(Which none without remorse forsake,)
    Of truth and innocence.

  " O Father, hear me patiently!"
    The blushing Maiden said;
  " I tremble, Father, while I speak;
    But surely not for dread!

  " If all my wishes have till now
    Found favour in thy sight,

And ever to perform thy will
Hath been my best delight,
Why should I fear to tell thee now
The visions of this night?

" I stood in a dream at the altar,..
But it was as an earthly Bride;
. And Eleëmon thy freedman
Was the Bridegroom at my side.

" Thou, Father, gavest me to him,
With thy free and full consent;
And,.. why should I dissemble it?..
Methought I was content.

" Months then and years were crowded
In the course of that busy night;
I claspt a baby to my breast,
And, oh! with what delight!

" Yea, I was fruitful as a Vine;
Our heavenly Parent me and mine
   In all things seem'd to bless ;
Our ways were ways of peace, our paths
   Were paths of pleasantness.

" When I taught lisping lips to pray,
   The joy it was to me,
O Father, thus to train these plants
   For immortality !

" I saw their little winning ways
   Their grandsire's love engage ;
Methought they were the pride, the joy,
   The crown of his old age.

" When from the vision I awoke,
   A voice was in my ear,..

D

A waking voice,.. I heard it twice;
    No human tongue was near;

" No human utterance so could reach
    The secret soul, no human speech
        So make the soul rejoice;
    In hearing it I felt and knew
        It was an Angel's voice!

" And thus in words distinct it said,
      ' So, Cyra, must it be!
    The duties of a wedded life
    Hath Heaven ordain'd for thee.' "

Her cheek was like the new-blown rose,
    While thus she told her tale;
    Proterius listened earnestly,
    And as he heard grew pale.

For he, too, in the dreams of night
At the altar had seem'd to stand,
And to Eleëmon his freedman
Had given his daughter's hand.

Their offspring, courting his caress,
About his knees had throng'd;
A lovely progeny, in whom,
When he was in the silent tomb,
His line should be prolong'd.

And he had heard a waking voice,
Which said it so must be,
Pronouncing upon Cyra's name
A holiest eulogy:

" Her shall her husband praise, and her
Her children blest shall call:
Many daughters have done virtuously,
But thine excelleth them all!"

No marvel if his heart were moved;
  The dream he saw was one:
He kiss'd his trembling child, and said,
  " The will of Heaven be done!"

Little did child or sire in this
  The work of sorcery fear!
As little did Eleëmon think
That the hand of Heaven was here.

IV.

FROM house to house, from street to street
　　The rapid rumour flies;
Incredulous ears it found, and hands
　　Are lifted in surprise;
And tongues thro' all the astonished town
　　Are busier now than eyes.

" So sudden and so strange a change!
　　A Freedman, too, the choice!
The shame,..the scandal,..and for what?
　　A vision and a voice!

" Had she not chosen the strait gate,..
The narrow way,..the holy state,..
　　The Sanctuary's abode?

Would Heaven call back its votary
To the broad and beaten road?

" To carnal wishes would it turn
The mortified intent?
For this are miracles vouchsafed!
For this are Angels sent!

" A plain collusion! a device
Between the girl and youth!
Good easy man must the Father be,
To take such tale for truth!"

So judged the acrid and the austere,
And they whose evil heart
Inclines them, in whate'er betides,
To take the evil part.

But others, whom a kindlier frame

To better thoughts inclined,
Preserved, amid their wonderment,
An equitable mind.

They would not of Proterius thus
Injuriously misdeem,..
A grave, good man, and with the wise
For wisdom in esteem.

No easy ear, or vain belief,
Would he to falsehood lend;
Nor ever might light motive him
From well-weighed purpose bend.

And surely on his pious child,
The gentle Cyra, meek and mild,
Could no suspicion rest;
For in this daughter he had been
Above all fathers blest.

As dutiful as beautiful,
Her praise was widely known,
Being one who, as she grew in years,
Had still in goodness grown.

And what tho' Eleëmon were
A man of lowly birth?
Enough it was if Nature had
Ennobled him with worth.

" This was no doubtful thing," they said,
" For he had in the house been bred,
Nor e'er from thence removed;
But there from childhood had been known,
And trusted and approved.

" Such as he was his qualities
Might to the world excuse
The Maid and Father for their choice,

. Without the vision and the voice,
  Had they been free to choose.

" But Heaven by miracle had made
    Its pleasure manifest;   -
  That manifested will must set
  All doubtful thoughts to rest.
Mysterious tho' they be, the ways
    Of Providence are best."

The wondering City thus discoursed;
    To Abibas alone
The secret truth, and even to him
  But half the truth, was known.

Meantime the Church hath been prepared
    For spousal celebration;
  The Sisters to their cells retire,
    Amazed at such mutation.

The habit and hood of camel's hair,
Which with the sacred scissars there
 On the altar were display'd,
Are taken thence, and in their stead
 The marriage rings are laid.

Behold, in garments gay with gold,
 For other spousals wrought,
The Maiden from her Father's house
 With bridal pomp is brought.

And now before the Holy Door
 In the Ante-nave they stand;
The Bride and Bridegroom side by side,
The Paranymphs in festal pride
 Arranged on either hand.

Then from the Sanctuary the Priests,
 With incense burning sweet,

Advance, and at the Holy Door
The Bride and Bridegroom meet.

There to the Bride and Bridegroom they
The marriage tapers gave;
And to the altar as they go,
With cross-way movement to and fro,
The thuribule they wave.

For fruitfulness, and perfect love,
And constant peace, they prayed,
On Eleëmon, the Lord's Servant,
And Cyra, the Lord's Handmaid.

They call'd upon the Lord to bless
Their spousal celebration,
And sanctify the marriage tie
To both their souls' salvation.

A pause at every prayer they made,
Whereat with one accord
The Choristers took up their part,
And sung in tones that thrilled the heart,
Have mercy on us, Lord!

Then with the marriage rings the Priest
Betrothed them each to each,
And, as the sacred pledge was given,
Resumed his awful speech;

Pronouncing them before high Heaven
This hour espoused to be,
Now and for ever more, for time
And for eternity.

This did he in the presence
Of Angels and of men:

And at every pause the Choristers
　Intoned their deep Amen!

Then to that gracious Lord, the Priest
　　His supplication made,
Who, as our sacred Scriptures tell,
　Did bring Rebecca to the well
When Abraham's servant prayed.

He call'd upon that gracious Lord
　　To stablish with his power
The espousals made between them,
　In truth and love, this hour;

And with his mercy and his word
　Their lot, now link'd, to bless,
And let his Angel guide them
　In the way of righteousness.

With a Christian benediction,
The Priest dismist them then,
And the Choristers, with louder voice,
Intoned the last Amen!

The days of Espousals are over:
And on the Crowning-day,
To the sacred fane the bridal train,
A gay procession, take again
Thro' thronging streets their way.

Before them, by the Paranymphs,
The coronals are borne,
Composed of all sweet flowers of spring
By virgin hands that morn.

With lighted tapers in array
They enter the Holy Door,

And the Priest with the waving thuribule
  Perfumes the way before.

He raised his voice, and call'd aloud
  On Him who from the side
Of our first Father, while he slept,
  Form'd Eve to be his bride;

Creating Woman thus for Man
  A helpmate meet to be,
For youth and age, for good and ill,
For weal and woe, united still
  In strict society;

Flesh of his flesh, appointing them
  One flesh to be, one heart:
Whom God hath joined together
  Them let not man dispart!

And on our Lord he call'd, by whom
The marriage feast was blest,
When first by miracle he made
His glory manifest.

Then in the ever-blessed Name,
Almighty over all,
From the man's Paranymph he took
The marriage coronal ;

And crowning him therewith, in that
Thrice holy Name, he said,
" Eleëmon, the Servant of God, is crown'd
For Cyra, the Lord's Handmaid !"

Next, with like action and like words,
Upon her brow he set
Her coronal, intwin'd wherein
The rose and lily met;

How beautifully they beseem'd,
　　Her locks of glossy jet!

Her he for Eleëmon crown'd
　The Servant of the Lord,..
Alas, how little did that name
　With his true state accord!

" Crown them with honour, Lord!" he said,
" With blessings crown the righteous head!
　　To them let peace be given,
　　A holy life, a hopeful end,
　　A heavenly crown in Heaven!"

Still as he made each separate prayer
For blessings that they in life might share,
　　And for their eternal bliss,
　　The echoing Choristers replied,
　　" O Lord, so grant thou this!"

E

How differently meantime, before
The altar as they knelt,
While they the sacred rites partake
Which endless matrimony make,
The Bride and Bridegroom felt!

She, who possest her soul in peace
And thoughtful happiness,
With her whole heart had inly join'd
In each devout address.

His lips the while had only moved
In hollow repetition;
For he had steel'd himself, like one
Bound over to perdition.

In present joy he wrapt his heart,
And resolutely cast
All other thoughts beside him,
Of the future, or the past.

V.

TWELVE years have held their quiet course
　　Since Cyra's nuptial day:
　　How happily, how rapidly,
　　Those years have past away!

Blest in her husband she hath been;
　　He loved her as sincerely,
　　(Most sinful and unhappy man!)
　　As he had bought her dearly.

She hath been fruitful as a vine,
　　And in her children blest;
Sorrow hath not come near her yet,
Nor fears to shake, nor cares to fret,
　　Nor grief to wound the breast.

E 2

And blest alike would her husband be,
Were all things as they seem;
Eleëmon hath every earthly good,
And with every man's esteem.

But where the accursed reed had drawn
The heart-blood from his breast,
A small red spot remain'd
Indelibly imprest.

Nor could he from his heart throw off
The consciousness of his state;
It was there with a dull, uneasy sense,
A coldness and a weight;

It was there when he lay down at night,
It was there when at morn he rose:
He feels it whatever he does,
It is with him wherever he goes.

No occupation from his mind
That constant sense can keep;
It is present in his waking hours,
It is present in his sleep;

But still he felt it most,
And with painfullest weight it prest,..
O miserable man!
When he was happiest.

O miserable man,
Who hath all the world to friend,
Yet dares not in prosperity
Remember his latter end!

But happy man, whate'er
His earthly lot may be,
Who looks on Death as the Angel
That shall set his spirit free,

And bear it to its heritage
Of immortality!

In such faith hath Proterius lived;
And strong is that faith and fresh,
As if obtaining then new power,
When he hath reach'd the awful hour
Appointed for all flesh.

Eleëmon and his daughter
With his latest breath he blest,
And saying to them, " we shall meet
Again before the Mercy-seat!"
Went peacefully to rest.

This is the balm which God
Hath given for every grief;
And Cyra, in her anguish,
Look'd heavenward for relief.

But her miserable husband
Heard a voice within him say,
" Eleëmon, Eleëmon,
Thou art sold to the Demon!"
And his heart seem'd dying away.

Whole Cæsarea is pour'd forth
To see the funeral state,
When Proterius is borne to his resting-place
Without the Northern Gate.

Not like a Pagan's is his bier
At doleful midnight borne
By ghastly torchlight, and with wail
Of women hired to mourn.

With tapers in the face of day,
These rites their faithful hope display;
In long procession slow,

With hymns that fortify the heart,
And prayers that soften woe.

In honour of the dead man's rank,
But of his virtues more,
The holy Bishop Basil
Was one the bier who bore.

And with the Bishop side by side,
As nearest to the dead allied,
Was Eleëmon seen:
All mark'd, but none could rede aright,
The trouble in his mien.

" His master's benefits on him
Were well bestowed," they said,
" Whose sorrow now full plainly showed
How well he loved the dead."

They little ween'd what thoughts in him
   The solemn psalm awoke,
Which to all other hearts that hour
   Its surest comfort spoke:

" Gather my Saints together:
   In peace let them be laid,
They who with me," thus saith the Lord,
   " Their covenant have made !"

What pangs to Eleëmon then,
O wretchedest of wretched men,
   That psalmody conveyed !
For conscience told him that he too
   A covenant had made.

And when he would have closed his ears
   Against the unwelcome word,

Then from some elms beside the way
A Raven's croak was heard.

To him it seem'd a hollow voice
That warn'd him of his doom;
For the tree whereon the Raven sate
Grew over the Pagan's tomb.

VI.

WHEN weariness would let her
No longer pray and weep,
And midnight long was past,
Then Cyra fell asleep.

Into that wretched sleep she sunk
Which only sorrow knows,
Wherein the exhausted body rests,
But the heart hath no repose.

Of her Father she was dreaming,
Still aware that he was dead,
When, in the visions of the night,
He stood beside her bed.

Crown'd, and in robes of light he came;
She saw he had found grace;
And yet there seem'd to be
A trouble in his face.

The eye and look were still the same
That she from her cradle knew;
And he put forth his hand, and blest her,
As he had been wont to do.

But then the smile benign
Of love forsook his face,
And a sorrowful displeasure
Came darkly in its place;

And he cast on Eleëmon
A melancholy eye,
And sternly said, " I bless thee not, ..
Bondsman! thou knowest why!"

Again to Cyra then he turn'd,
" Let not thy husband rest,
Till he hath wash'd away with tears
The red spot from his breast!

" Hold fast thy hope, and Heaven will not
Forsake thee in thine hour:
Good Angels will be near thee,
And Evil ones shall fear thee,
And Faith will give thee power."

Perturb'd, yet comforted, she woke,
For in her waking ear
The words were heard which promised her
A strength above all fear.

An odour, that refresh'd no less
Her spirit with its blessedness
Than her corporeal frame,

Was breathed around, and she surely found
That from Paradise it came.

And, tho' the form revered was gone,
A clear, unearthly light
Remain'd, encompassing the bed,
When all around was night.

It narrowed as she gazed;
And soon she saw it rest,
Concentered, like an eye of light,
Upon her husband's breast.

Not doubting now the presence
Of some good presiding power,
Collectedness as well as strength
Was given her in this hour.

And rising half, the while in deep

But troubled sleep he lay,
She drew the covering from his breast
    With cautious hand away.

The small round blood-red mark she saw;
    Eleëmon felt her not;
But in his sleep he groan'd, and cried
    " Out! out... accursed spot!"

The darkness of surrounding night
Closed then upon that eye of light.
    She waited for the break
Of day, and lay the while in prayer
    For that poor sinner's sake...

In fearful, miserable prayer;
But while she pray'd the load of care
    Less heavily bore on her heart,
And light was given, enabling her
    To choose her difficult part.

And she drew, as comfortable texts
    Unto her thoughts recurr'd,
Refreshment from the living well
    Of God's unerring word.

But when the earliest dawn appear'd,
    Herself in haste she array'd,
And watch'd his waking patiently,
    And still as she watch'd she pray'd;
And when Eleëmon had risen,
    She spake to him, and said:

" We have been visited this night!!
    My Father's Ghost I have seen;
I heard his voice,..an awful voice!..
    And so hast thou, I ween!"

Eleëmon was pale when he awoke;
    But paler then he grew,

And over his whole countenance
There came a deathlike hue.

Still he controul'd himself, and sought
Her question to beguile ;
And forcing, while he answered her,
A faint and hollow smile, ..

" Cyra," he said, " thy thoughts possest
With one too painful theme,
Their own imaginations
For reality misdeem ;
Let not my dearest, best beloved,
Be troubled for a dream !" .

" O Eleëmon," she replied,
" Dissemble not with me thus !
Ill it becomes me to forget
What dreams have been to us !

F

" Thinkest thou there can be peace for me,
    Near to me as thou art,
While some unknown and fearful sin
    Is festering at thy heart?

" Eleëmon, Eleëmon,
    I may not let thee rest,
Till thou hast wash'd away with tears
    The red spot from thy breast!

" Thus to conceal thy crime from me,
    It is no tenderness!
The worst is better known than fear'd.
    Whatever it be, confess;
And the Merciful will cleanse thee
    From all unrighteousness!"

Like an aspen leaf he trembled;
    And his imploring eye

Bespake compassion, ere his lips
Could utter their dreaded reply.

" O dearly loved, as dearly bought,
My sin and punishment I had thought
      To bear thro' life alone :
Too much the Vision hath reveal'd,
      And all must now be known !.

" On thee, methinks, and only thee
      Dare I for pity call :
Abhor me not... renounce me not,..
      My life, my love, my all !

. " And Cyra, sure if ever cause
      Might be a sinner's plea,
'Twould be for that lost wretch who sold
      . His hope of Heaven for thee !

Thou seest a miserable man
Given over to despair,
Who has bound himself by his act and deed
To the Prince of the Powers of the Air."

She seized him by the arm,
And hurrying him into the street,
" Come with me to the Church," she cried,
" And to Basil the Bishop's feet!"

VII.

PUBLIC must be the sinner's shame
As heinous his offence;
So Basil said, when he ordain'd
His form of penitence.

And never had such dismay been felt
Thro' that astonished town,
As when, at morn, the Cryer went
Proclaiming up and down,

" The miserable sinner, Eleëmon,
Who for love hath sold himself to the Demon,
His guilt before God and man declares;
And beseeches all good Christians
To aid him with their prayers."

Many were the hearts compassionate
Whom that woeful petition moved;
For he had borne his fortune meekly,
And therefore was well beloved.

Open his hand had been,
And liberal of its store;
And the prayers of the needy arose
Who had daily been fed at his door.

They too whom Cyra's secret aid
Relieved from pressing cares,
In this, her day of wretchedness,
Repaid her with their prayers.

And from many a gentle bosom
Supplications for mercy were sent,
If haply they might aid
The wretched penitent.

Sorely such aid he needed then!,
Basil himself, of living men
The powerfullest in prayer,
For pity, rather than in hope,
Had bidden him not despair.

So hard a thing for him it seem'd
To wrest from Satan's hand
The fatal Bond, which, while retain'd,
Must against him in judgement stand.

" Dost thou believe," he said, " that Grace
Itself can reach this grief?"
With a feeble voice, and a woeful eye,
" Lord, I believe!" was the sinner's reply,
" Help thou mine unbelief!"

The Bishop then crost him on the brow,
And crost him on the breast:

And told him if he did his part
With true remorse and faithful heart,
God's mercy might do the rest.

" Alone in the holy Relic-room
Must thou pass day and night,
And wage with thy ghostly enemies
A more than mortal fight.

" The trial may be long, and the struggle strong,
Yet be not thou dismay'd;
For thou mayest count on Saints in Heaven,
And on earthly prayers for aid.

" And in thy mind this scripture bear
With stedfast faithfulness, whate'er
To appall thee may arrive;
' When the wicked man turneth away from his sin
He shall save his soul alive!'

" Take courage as thou lookest around
   On the relics of the blest;
And night and day continue to pray,
Until thy tears have wash'd away
   The stigma from thy breast!"

" Let me be with him!" Cyra cried;
   " If thou mayest not be there,
   In this sore trial I at least
My faithful part may bear:

" My presence may some comfort prove,
   Yea, haply some defence;
   O Father, in myself I feel
   The strength of innocence!"

" Nay Daughter, nay; it must not be!
   Tho' dutiful this desire;
He may, by Heaven's good grace, be saved,
   But only as if by fire!

" Sights which should never meet thine eye
Before him may appear :
And fiendish voices proffer words
Which should never assail thy ear.
Alone must he this trance sustain ;
Keep thou thy vigils here !"

He led him to the Relic-room ;
Alone he left him there ;
And Cyra with the Nuns remain'd
To pass her time in prayer.

Alone was Eleëmon left
For mercy on Heaven to call ;
Deep and unceasing were his prayers,
But not a tear would fall.

His lips were parch'd, his head was hot,
His eyeballs throbb'd with heat ;

And in that utter silence
He could hear his temples beat.

But cold his feet, and cold his hands ;
And at his heart there lay
An icy coldness unrelieved,
While he prayed the livelong day :

A long, long day !   It past away
In dreadful expectation ;
Yet free throughout the day was he
From outward molestation.

Nor sight appear'd, nor voice was heard,
Tho' every moment both he fear'd ;
The Spirits of the Air
Where busy the while in infusing
Suggestions of despair.

And he in strong endeavour still
Against them strove with earnest will;
Heart-piercing was his cry,
Heart-breathed his groaning; but it seem'd
That the source of tears was dry.

And now had evening closed;
The dim lamp light alone
On the stone cross, and the marble walls,
And the shrines of the Martyrs, shone.

Before the Cross Eleëmon lay;
His knees were on the ground;
Courage enough to touch the Cross
Itself, he had not found.

But on the steps of the pedestal
His lifted hands were laid;

And in that lowliest attitude
The suffering sinner pray'd.

A strong temptation of the Fiend,
Which bade him despair and die,
He with the aid of Scripture
Had faithfully put by;
And then, as with a dawning hope,
He raised this contrite cry:

" Oh that mine eyes were fountains!
If the good grace of Heaven
Would give me tears, methinks I then
Might hope to be forgiven!"

To that meek prayer a short loud laugh
From fiendish lips replied:
Close at his ear he felt it,
And it sounded on every side.

From the four walls and the vaulted roof
A shout of mockery rung;
And the echoing ground repeated the sound,
Which peal'd above, and below, and around,
From many a fiendish tongue.

The lamps went out at that hideous shout;
But darkness had there no place,
For the room was fill'd with a lurid light
That came from a Demon's face.

A dreadful face it was, .. too well
By Eleëmon known!
Alas! he had seen it when he stood
Before the dolorous throne.

" Eleëmon! Eleëmon!"
Sternly said the Demon,
" How have I merited this?

I kept my covenant with thee,
And placed thee in worldly bliss.

" And still thou mightest have had,
Thine after days to bless,
Health, wealth, long life, and whatsoe'er
The World calls happiness.

" Fool, to forego thine earthly joys,
Who hast no hope beyond!
For judgement must be given for me,
When I sue thee upon the Bond.

" Remember I deceived thee not ;
Nor had I tempted thee ;
Thou camest of thine own accord,
And didst act knowingly!

" I told thee thou mightest vainly think

To cheat me by contrition,
When thou wert written down among
The Children of Perdition!

" ' So help me, Satan!' were thy words
When thou didst this allow;
I help'd thee, Eleëmon, then, . .
And I will have thee now!"

At the words of the Fiend, from the floor
Eleëmon in agony sprung; ·
Up the steps of the pedestal he ran,
And to the Cross he clung.

And then it seem'd as if he drew,
While he claspt the senseless stone,
A strength he had not felt till then,
A hope he had not known.

So when the Demon ceased,
He answered him not a word;
But looking upward, he
His faithful prayer preferr'd:

" All, all, to Thee, my Lord
And Saviour, I confess!
And I know that Thou canst cleanse me
From all unrighteousness!

" I have turned away from my sin!
In Thee do I put my trust!
To such Thou hast promised forgiveness,
And Thou art faithful and just!"

With that the Demon disappear'd;
The lamps resumed their light;
Nor voice, nor vision more
Disturb'd him thro' the night.

He stirr'd not from his station,
But there stood fix'd in prayer;
And when Basil the Bishop enter'd
At morn, he found him there.

VIII.

WELL might the Bishop see what he
Had undergone that night;
Remorse and agony of mind
Had made his dark hair white.

So should the inner change, he ween'd,
With the outward sign accord;
And holy Basil crost himself,
And blest our gracious Lord.

" Well hast thou done," said he, " my son,
And faithfully fought the fight;
So shall this day compleat, I trust,
The victory of the night.

G 2

" I fear'd that forty days and nights
    Too little all might be;
But great and strange hath been the change
    One night hath wrought in thee."

" O Father, Father!" he replied,
    " And hath it been but one?
An endless time it seem'd to me!
    I almost thought Eternity
    With me had been begun.

" And surely this poor flesh and blood
Such terrors could not have withstood,
    If grace had not been given;
But when I claspt the blessed Cross,
    I then had help from Heaven.

" The coldness from my heart is gone;
    But still the weight is there,

And thoughts which I abhor, will come
And tempt me to despair.

" Those thoughts I constantly repell;
And all, methinks, might yet be well,
Could I but weep once more,
And with true tears of penitence
My dreadful state deplore.

" Tears are denied; their source is dried!
And must it still be so?
O Thou, who from a rock didst make
The living waters flow,

" A broken and a bleeding heart
This hour I offer Thee;
And, when Thou seest good, my tears
Shall then again be free!"

A knocking at the door was heard
As he ended this reply;
Hearing that unexpected sound,
The Bishop turn'd his eye,
And his venerable Mother,
Emmelia the Abbess, drew nigh.

" We have not ceased this mournful night,"
Said she, " on Heaven to call:
And our afflicted Cyra
Hath edified us all.

" More fervent prayers from suffering heart,
I ween, have ne'er been sent;
And now she asks, as some relief,
In this, her overwhelming grief,
To see the penitent.

" So earnestly she ask'd, that I

Her wish would not defer;
And I have brought her to the door,
Forgive me, Son, if I err."

" Hard were I did I not consent
To thy compassionate intent,
O Mother," he replied;
And raising then his voice, " Come in,
Thou innocent!" he cried.

That welcome word when Cyra heard,
With a sad pace and slow,
Forward she came, like one whose heart
Was overcharged with woe.

Her face was pale, .. long illness would
Have changed those features less:
And long-continued tears had dimm'd
Her eyes with heaviness.

Her husbands words had reach'd her ear
  When at the door she stood;
" Thou hast prayed in vain for tears," she said,
  " While I have pour'd a flood!

" Mine flow, and they will flow; they must;
  They cannot be represt!
And oh that they might wash away
  The stigma from thy breast!

" Oh that these tears might cleanse that spot, . .
  Tears which I cannot check!"
Profusely weeping as she spake,
  She fell upon his neck.

He claspt the mourner close, and in
  That passionate embrace,
In grief for her, almost forgot
  His own tremendous case.

Warm as they fell he felt her tears,
        And in true sympathy,
So gracious Heaven permitted then,
    His own to flow were free.

And then the weight was taken off,
    Which at his heart had prest;..
O mercy! and the crimson spot
    Hath vanish'd from his breast!

At that most happy sight,
    The four with one accord
Fell on their knees, and blest
    The mercy of the Lord.

" What then! before the strife is done
        Would ye of victory boast?"
Said a Voice above: " they reckon too soon,
    Who reckon without their host!"

" Mine is he by a Bond
Which holds him fast in law:
I drew it myself for certainty,
And sharper than me must the Lawyer be
Who in it can find a flaw!

" Before the Congregation,
And in the face of day,
Whoever may pray, and whoever gainsay,
I will challenge him for my Bondsman,
And carry him quick away!"

" Ha, Satan! dost thou in thy pride,"
With righteous anger Basil cried,
" Defy the force of prayer?
In the face of the Church wilt thou brave it?
Why then we will meet thee there!

" There mayest thou set forth thy right,

With all thy might before the sight
Of all the Congregation:
And they that hour shall see the power
Of the Lord unto salvation!"

" A challenge fair! We meet then there,"
Rejoined the Prince of the Powers of the Air;
" The Bondsman is mine by right.
Let the whole city come at thy call:
And great and small, in face of them all,
I will have him in thy despite!"

So having said, he tarried not
To hear the Saint's reply.
" Beneath the sign which Constantine,"
Said Basil, " beheld in the sky,
We strive, and have our strength therein,
Therein our victory!"

IX.

THE Church is fill'd, so great the faith
That City in its Bishop hath;
And now the Congregation
Are waiting there in trembling prayer
And terrible expectation.

Emmelia and her Sisterhood
Have taken there their seat:
And Choristers and Monks and Priests,
And Psalmists there, and Exorcists,
Are stationed in order meet.

In sackcloth clad, with ashes strewn
Upon his whiter hair,
Before the steps of the altar,

His feet for penance bare,
Eleëmon stands, a spectacle
For men and Angels there.

Beside him Cyra stood, in weal
    Or woe, in good or ill,
Not to be severed from his side,
    His faithful helpmate still.

Dishevell'd were her raven locks,
    As one in mourner's guise;
And pale she was, but faith and hope
    Had now relumed her eyes.

At the altar Basil took his stand;
    He held the Gospel in his hand,
        And in his ardent eye
Sure trust was seen, and conscious power,
    And strength for victory.

At his command the Chorister
Enounced the Prophet's song,
" To God our Saviour mercies
And forgivenesses belong."

Ten thousand voices join'd to raise
The holy hymn on high,
And hearts were thrill'd and eyes were fill'd
By that full harmony.

And when they ceased, and Basil's hand
A warning signal gave,
The whole huge multitude was hush'd
In a stillness like that of the grave.

The Sun was high in a bright blue sky,
But a chill came over the crowd,
And the Church was suddenly darken'd,
As if by a passing cloud.

A sound as of a tempest rose,
Tho' the day was calm as clear;
Intrepid must the heart have been
Which did not then feel fear.

In the sound of the storm came the dreadful Form;
The Church then darken'd more,
And He was seen erect on the screen
Over the Holy Door.

Day-light had sickened at his sight;
And the gloomy presence threw
A shade profound over all around,
Like a cheerless twilight hue.

" I come hither," said the Demon,
" For my Bondsman Eleëmon!
Mine is he, body and soul.
See all men!" and with that on high
He held the open scroll.

The fatal signature appear'd
To all the multitude,
Distinct as when the accursed pen
Had traced it with fresh blood.
" See all men!" Satan cried again,
And then his claim pursued.

" I ask for justice!　I prefer
An equitable suit!
I appeal to the Law, and the case
Admitteth of no dispute. ·

" If there be justice here,
If Law have place in Heaven,
Award upon this Bond
Must then for me be given.

" What to my rightful claim,
Basil, canst thou gainsay,

That I should not seize the Bondsman,
    And carry him quick away?

" The writing is confess'd;..
No plea against it shown;..
    The forfeiture is mine,
    And now I take my own !"

" Hold there!" cried Basil, with a voice
    That arrested him on his way,
When from the screen he would have swoopt
    To pounce upon his prey;

" Hold there, I say!   Thou canst not sue
    Upon this Bond by law!
    A sorry legalist were he
Who could not in thy boasted plea
    Detect its fatal flaw.

H

"The Deed is null, for it was framed
With fraudulent intent;
A thing unlawful in itself;
A wicked instrument,..
Not to be pleaded in the Courts...
Sir Fiend thy cause is shent!

" This were enough; but,'more than this,
A maxim, as thou knowest, it is
Whereof all Laws partake,
That no one may of his own wrong
His own advantage make.

" The man, thou sayest, thy Bondsman is:
Mark now, how stands the fact!
Thou hast allowed,..nay, aided him
As a Freedman to contract
A marriage with this Christian woman here,
And by a public act.

" That act being publicly perform'd
    With thy full cognizance,
Claim to him as thy Bondsman thou
    Canst never more advance.

" For when they solemnly were then
United, in sight of Angels and men,
    The matrimonial band
Gave to the wife a right in him;
    And we on this might stand.

" Thy claim upon the man was by
    Thy silence then forsaken;
A marriage thus by thee procured
    May not by thee be shaken;
And thou, O Satan, as thou seest,
    In thine own snare art taken!"

So Basil said, and paused awhile;
    H 2

The Arch-Fiend answered not;
But he heaved in vexation
A sulphurous sigh for the Bishop's vocation,
And thus to himself he thought;

" The Law thy calling ought to have been,
With thy wit so ready, and tongue so free!
To prove by reason in reason's despite,
That right is wrong, and wrong is right,
And white is black, and black is white,..
What a loss have I had in thee!"

" I rest not here," the Saint pursued;
" Tho' thou in this mayest see,
That in the meshes of thine own net
I could entangle thee!

Fiend! thou thyself didst bring about
The spousal celebration,

Which link'd them by the nuptial tie
For both their souls' salvation.

" Thou sufferedst them before high Heaven
With solemn rights espoused to be,
Then and for evermore, for time
        And for eternity.

    " That tie holds good; those rites
    Will reach their whole intent,
    And thou of his salvation wert
        Thyself the instrument.

" And now, methinks, thou seest in this
    A higher power than thine;
And that thy ways were overruled,
    To work the will divine !"

With rising energy he spake,

And more majestic look;
And with authoritative hand
Held forth the Sacred Book.

Then with a voice of power he said,
" The Bond is null and void!
It is nullified, as thou knowest well,
By a Covenant whose strength by Hell
Can never be destroyed!

" The Covenant of Grace,
That greatest work of Heaven,
Which whoso claims in perfect faith,
His sins shall be forgiven!

" Were they as scarlet red
They should be white as wool;
This is the All-mighty's Covenant,
Who is All-merciful!

" His Minister am I !
In his All-mighty name
To this repentant sinner
God's pardon I proclaim !

" In token that against his soul
The sin shall no longer stand,
The writing is effaced, which there
Thou holdest in thy hand !

" Angels that are in bliss above
This triumph of Redeeming Love
Will witness, and rejoice ;
And ye shall now in thunder hear
Heaven's ratifying voice !"

A peal of thunder shook the pile ;
The Church was fill'd with light,
And when the flash was past, the Fiend
Had vanished from their sight.

He fled as he came, but in anger and shame,
The pardon was compleat,
. And the impious scroll was dropt, a blank,
At Eleëmon's feet.

NOTES

TO

ALL FOR LOVE.

FROM THE LIFE OF S. BASIL THE GREAT, BY
S. AMPHILOCHIUS, BISHOP OF ICONIUM.
Rosweyde, Vitæ Patrum, pp. 156. 158.

/ / ( )

————

" *Helladius autem sanctæ recordationis, qui inspector et minister fuit miraculorum quæ ab eo patrata sunt, quique post obitum ejusdem Apostolicæ memoriæ Basilii sedem illius suscipere meruit, vir miraculis et clarus, atque omni virtute ornatus, retulit mihi, quia cùm senator quidam fidelis, nomine Proterius pergeret ad sancta et percolenda . loca, et ibidem filiam suam tondere, et in unum venerabilium monasteriorum mittere, et sacrificium Deo offerre voluisset ; diabolus, qui ab initio homicida est, invidens ejus religioso proposito, commovit unum ex servis ejus, et hunc ad puellæ succendit amorem. Hic itaque cùm tanto voto esset indignus, et non auderet propositum saltem contingere, alloquitur unum ex detestandis maleficis, repromittens illi, ut si fortè arte suâ posset illam commovere, multam ei auri tribueret quantitatem. At verò veneficus dixit ad eum : O homo, ego ad hoc impos existo : sed si vis, mitto te ad provisorem meum diabolum, et ille faciet voluntatem tuam, si tu dumtaxat feceris voluntatem ejus. Qui dixit ad eum : Quæcunque dixerit mihi, faciam.*   *Ait ille :*   *Abrenuntias, inquit, Christo in scriptis ?*   *Dicit ei : Etiam.*   *Porrò iniquitatis operarius dicit ei :   Si ad hoc paratus es, co-operator tibi efficiar. Ille autem ad ipsum : Paratus sum, tantùm ut consequar desiderium. Et factá epistolá, pessimæ operationis minister ad diabolum destinavit eam, habentem dictatum hujusmodi : Quoniam domino et provisori meo oportet me dare operam, quò a Christianorum religione discedant, et ad tuam societatem accedant, ut compleatur portio tua ; misi tibi præsentem, meas deferentem litterulas, cupidine puellæ sauciatum. Et obsecro ut hujus voti compos existat, ut et in hoc glorior, et cum affluentiori alacritate colligam amatores tuos. Et datá ei epistolá, dixit : Vade tali horá noctis, et sta supra monumentum alicujus pagani, et erige chartam in aëra, et adstabunt tibi, qui te debent ducere ad diabolum. Qui hoc alacriter gesto, emisit miserrimam illam vocem, invocans diaboli adjutorium : et continuò adstiterunt ei principes potestatis tenebrarum, spiritus nequitiæ, et suscepto qui fuerat deceptus, cum gaudio magno duxerunt eum ubi erat diabolus, quem et monstraverunt ei super excelsum solium sedentem, et in gyro ejus nequitiæ spiritus circumstantes ; et susceptis venefici litteris, dixit ad infelicem illum : Credis in me ? Qui dixit : Credo. Dixit ei diabolus : Tergiversatores estis vos Christiani, et quidem quando me opus habetis, venitis ad me ; cùm autem consecuti fueritis affectum, abnegatis me et acceditis ad Christum vestrum, qui, cùm sit bonus atque misericors, suscipit vos.*

Sed fac mihi in scriptis tam Christi tui et sancti Baptis-
matis voluntariam abrenuntiationem, quàm in me per
sæcula spontaneam repromissionem, et quia mecum eris
in die judicii simul perfruiturus æternis suppliciis, quæ
mihi sunt præparata. At ille exposuit propriæ manus
scriptum, quemadmodum fuerat expetitus. Rursusque
ille corruptor animarum draco destinat dæmones fornica-
tioni præpositos, et exardescere faciunt puellam ad amorem
pueri, quæ projecit se in pavimentum, et cæpit clamare ad
patrem: Miserere mei, miserere: quia atrociter torqueor
propter talem puerum nostrum! Compatere visceribus
tuis; ostende in me unigenitam tuam paternum affectum, et
junge me puero, quem elegi. Quòd si hæc agere nolueris,
videbis me amarâ morte post paululum mortuam, et ratio-
nem dabis Deo pro me in die judicii. Pater. autem cum
lachrymis dicebat: Heu mihi peccatori! quid est quod
contigit miseræ filiæ meæ? quis thesaurum meum furatus
est? quis filiæ meæ injuriam intulit? quis dulce oculorum
meorum lumen exstinxit? ego te semper supercælesti
sponso consiliatus sum desponsare Christo, et Angelorum
contubernio sociam constituere, et in psalmis et hymnis
et canticis spiritualibus canere Deo accelerabam: tu
autem in lasciviam petulantiæ insanisti! Dimitte me,
sicut volo, cum Deo contractum facere, ne deducas senec-
tutem meam cum mærore in infernum, neque confusione
nobilitatem parentum tuorum operias. Quæ in nihilum
reputans, quæ à patre sibi dicebantur, perseverabat cla-
mans: Pater mi, aut fac desiderium meum, aut priùs

*pauxillùm mortuam me videbis. Pater itaque ejus in
magná dementatione constitutus, tam immensitate mœsti-
tiœ absorptus, quàm amicorum consiliis acquiescens se ad-
monentium, ac dicentium, expedire potiùs voluntatem
puellæ fieri, quàm sese manibus interficere, consensit, et
præcepit fieri desiderium puellæ potiùs, quàm eam exitia-
bili tradere morti. Et mox protulit puerum qui quære-
batur, simul et propriam genitam, et dans eis omnia bona
sua, dixit: Salve nata vere misera ; nnultum lumentaberis
repœnitens in novissimis, quando nihil tibi proderit.
Porrò nefandi matrimonii conjugio facto, et diabolicæ
operationis completo facinore, et pauco tempore pretere-
unte, notatus est puer à quibusdam, quòd non ingrederetur
ecclesiam, neque attrectaret immortalia et vivifica Sacra-
menta, et dicunt miserandæ uxori ejus: Noveris quia
maritus tuus, quem elegisti, non est Christianus, sed
extraneus est à fide, et penitùs est alienus. Quæ tenebris
et dirá plagá referta, projecit se in pavimentum, et cœpit
ungulis semetipsam discerpere, et percutere pectus, atque
clamare : Nemo umquam qui parentibus inobediens fuit,
salvus factus est. Quis annuntiabit patri meo confusio-
nem meam? Heu mihi infelici! in quod perditionis
profundum descendi! quare nata sum? vel nata quare
non statim indireptibilis facta sum? Hujusmodi ergo
eam complorantem seductus vir ejus agnoscens, venit ad
eam, asseverans non se ita rei veritatem habere: quæ in
refrigerium suasoriis ejus verbis deveniens, dixit ad eum:
Si vis mihi satisfacere, et infelicem animam meam certi-*

ficare, cras ego et tu pergemus unanimiter ad ecclesiam, et coram me sume intemerata mysteria, et taliter mihi poteris satisfacere. Tunc coactus dixit ei sententiam capituli. Protinus. ergo puella feminea infirmitate deposita, et consilio bono accepto, currit ad pastorem et discipulum Christi Basilium, adversus tantam clamans impietatem : *Misericordiam mihi miseræ præsta sancte Dei, miserere mei discipule Domini, quæ contractum cum dæmonibus feci. Miserere mei, quæ proprio patri facta sum inobediens. Et cognita illi fecit rei gestæ negotia.* Porrò sanctus Dei convocato puero, sciscitabatur ab eo si hæc hujusmodi essent. Qui ad sanctum cum lachrymis ait : *Etiam sancte Dei. Nam etsi ergo tacuero, opera mea clamabunt.* Et enarravit ei et ipse malignam diaboli operationem, qualiter ab exordio usque ad finem fuerit subsecutus. Tunc dicit ei : *Vis converti ad Dominum Deum nostrum?* Qui dixit : *Etiam volo, sed non possum.* Dicit ei : *Cur?* Respondit : *In scriptis abrenuntiavi Christo, et fœdus pepegi cum diabolo.* Dicit ei sanctus : *Non tibi sit curæ : benignus est Deus noster, et suscipiet te pœnitentiam agentem. Benignus enim est super malitiis nostris.* Et projiciens se puella ad pedes ejus, evangelice rogabat eum, dicens : *Discipule Christi Dei nostri, si quid potes, adjuva nos!* Dicit sanctus ad puerum : *Credis posse salvari?* At ille dixit : *Credo Domine, adjuva incredulitatem meam.* Et confestim adprehensâ manu ejus, et facto super eum Christi signo simul et oratione, retrusit illum in uno loco intra quem

*sacri habebantur amictus, et datá ei regulá oravit et ipse
pro illo per tres dies.   Post quos visitavit eum, et dixit ;
Quomodo te habes, fili?   Dicit ei puer : In magná sum,
domine, defectione.   Sancte Dei, non suffero clamores,
pavores, jacula, et lapidationes ipsorum.   Tenentes enim
propriæ manus meæ scripturam, objurgantur in me,
dicentes : Tu venisti ad nos, non nos ad te.   Et dicit
ei sanctus : Noli timere, fili mi, tantummodò crede.
Et datá ei modicá escá, et facto super eum Christi denuò
signo et oratione, inclusit eum ; et post paucos dies visitavit illum, et dixit : Quomodo te habes, fili?   Ait :
Pater sancte, à longe clamores eorum audio simul et
minas ; nam non video illos.   Et rursus dato ei cibo, et
effusá oratione clausit ostium, et discessit.   Prætereà
quadragesimo die abiit ad eum, et dicit illi : Quomodo te
habes, frater?   Respondit et dicit ei : Benè, sancte
Dei.   Vidi enim te hodie in somnio pugnantem pro me,
et vincentem diabolum.   Mox ergo secundùm consuetu-
dinem factá oratione eduxit illum, et duxit illum ad
cubiculum suum.*   Manè autem facto, convocato tam
venerabili clero, quam monasteriis et omni Christo ama-
bili populo, dixit eis : Filii mei dilecti, universi gratias
agamus Domino :   Ecce enim futurum est, et ovem per-
ditam pastor bonus super humeros suos imponat, et reducat
Ecclesiæ :   Et nos oportet pervigilem ducere noctem, et
deprecari voluntatem ipsius, ut non vincat corruptor
animarum.   Quo protinus acto, et promptissimè populo
congregato, per totam noctem uná cum bono pastore*

deprecati sunt Deum, cum lacrymis pro ipso clamantes,
Kyrie eleison. Et diluculò unà cum omni multitudine
populi assumit sanctus puerum, et tenens dexteram
manum ejus, duxit eum in sanctam Dei ecclesiam cum
psalmis et hymnis. Et ecce diabolus, qui vitæ nostræ
semper invidit, si hanc sine tristitiâ viderit, cum totâ
perniciosâ virtute suâ venit, et puero invisibiliter com-
prehenso, voluit rapere illum de manu sancti: et cæpit
puer clamans dicere: Sancte Dei auxiliare mihi, et adeà
contra illum impudenti instantiâ venit, ut ipsum egre-
gium Basilium simul cum illo impelleret et subverteret.
Conversus ergo sanctus ad diabolum ait: Impudentissime,
et animarum violator, pater tenebrarum et perditionis,
non tibi sufficit tua perditio, quam tibimet ipsi et his, qui
sub te sunt, acquisisti, sed adhuc non quiescis, et Dei mei
plasma tentando? Diabolus verò dixit ad eum: Præ-
judicas mihi, Basili: ita ut multi ex nobis audirent voces
ejus. At vero sanctus Dei ad eum: increpat, inquit,
tibi Dominus, diabole. At ille, Basili, præjudicium
mihi facis. Non ivi ego ad eum, sed ille venit ad me,
abrenuntiando Christum, mecumque est sponsione pactu-
atus, et ecce scriptum habeo, et in die judicii coram
communi judice deferam illud. Sanctus autem Domini
dixit: Benedictus Dominus Deus meus, non deponet
populus iste manus ab excelso cæli, nisi reddideris scrip-
tum. Et conversus dixit plebi: Tollite manus vestras
in cælum, universi clamantes cum lacrymis, Kyrie eleison.
Cumque staret populus horâ multâ extensas habentes

I

*manus in cælum, ecce scriptum pueri in aërem depor-
tatum, et ab omnibus visum venit, et positum est in
manus egregii patris nostri pastoris Basilii. Suscepto
autem illo, gratias egit Deo, gavisusque vehementer unâ
cum universâ plebe, dixit ad puerum : Recognoscis litterulas has, frater ? At ille dixit ad eum : Etiam sancte
Dei, propriæ manus meæ scriptura est. Et diruptâ
scripturâ introduxit eum in ecclesiam, et dignus habitus
est sacris interesse Missarum officiis, et participatione
sacrorum mysteriorum, et muneribus Christi. Et factâ
susceptione magna recreavit universum populum, et ducto
puero et instructo, atque datâ ei decenti regula, tradidit
eum uxori ejus, indesinenter glorificantem et laudantem
Deum. Amen.*

Baert, though he pronounces the life in which this legend appears to be apocryphal, does not deliver a decided opinion upon the legend itself. He says, " *Helladium Basilii in Episcopatu successorem fuisse, omnibus est indubitatum; vitam decessoris ab illo conscriptam, credimus (ut par est) S. Joanni Damasceno, qui utinam ad nos tantum transmisisset thesaurum; eum enim videtur præ oculis habuisse, cum locum inde unum descripsit in oratione pro sacris Imaginibus. An vero ea, quæ hic narrantur, ex Helladio sunt, lector judicet. Potuit enim fieri, ut eo quo Pseudo-Amphilochius scripsit tempore, fragmenta quædam Helladii extarent, quæ ipse retulerit in Basilium suum. Quod attinet ad Proterii filiam, a dæmone in amorem juvenis concitatam, simile quid contigisse B. Mariæ Antiochenæ referimus tomo 7 Maji, die 29, pag. 52. Mihi tamen verosimilius est, eumdèm qui Amphilochium mentitus est, mentiri etiam Helladium potuisse.*"—p. 952—3. Jun. t. 2.

The story, to which Baert refers, resembles the legend of St. Basil in one part, but is utterly unlike it in the circumstances wherein he has supposed the resemblance to exist. It appears to have been one of those fictions which were composed honestly as works of imagination, not like the lives of St. Benedict, St. Francis, St. Dominic, St. Ignatius Loyola, and so many of their respective orders, with a fraudulent intent, to impose upon mankind. Like other such fictions, however, it has been adopted and legitimated, by credulity and fraud, and the blessed Mary, the Virgin of Antioch, has her place accordingly in the Acta Sanctorum, on the 29th of May. But as the legend evidently was not written when Antioch was a Christian city, and moreover, as the legend itself contains nothing whatever by which its age could be determined, Papebroche presents it as *eo habendam esse loco, quo multa in Vitis Sanctorum Patrum, utilem quidem instructionem continentia ad formandos mores, sed ad historicam certitudinem parum aut nihil. Igitur istam quoque ut talem hic damus; liberum lectori relinquentes, ut eam quo volet gradu credibilitatis collocet.*

In this legend one of the chief persons in Antioch, Anthemius by name, failing to win the affections of Maria, who was the daughter of a poor widow, and had resolved to lead a life of celibacy, applies to a Magician to assist him. The Magician sends two Demons to influence mother and daughter in their sleep, so as to bring Maria to Anthemius's bed-chamber; but the temptations of worldly wealth, which are offered, have only the effect of alarming them; they rise in the middle of the night, and go toward the Church, there to pray for protection and deliverance: and on the way thither one Demon takes upon him Maria's form, while the other personates the mother, and thus decoys Maria into the apartment where Anthemius is expecting her. She is

however allowed to depart uninjured, upon a promise to
return at the end of fifteen days, and live with him as a
servant, provided he will offer her no violence... Nothing
can be more unlike the story of Proterius's daughter.
Having extorted an oath from her that she would return
according to this promise, Anthemius remains, wondering at the great power of the Magician. " Certes,"
thought he, " one who can do what he hath done in this
matter, is greater than all men; why, then, should I not
offer him all I am worth if he will make me equal to
himself?" And, being inflamed with this desire, he said
within himself, " If I were such as he is, whatever I
might wish for would be within my reach." This thought
came into his mind as if it were by Divine Providence,
to the end that he might willingly let the Virgin depart,
and that she might not be bound by the nefarious oath
which she had taken, and that the Devil, who was the
instigator of his evil desires, might be confounded in his
designs both upon the Virgin herself, and upon him who
was at this time the Virgin's enemy.

" As soon, therefore, as it was day, Anthemius went
out to seek for the Sorcerer, and to give him thanks.
Having found him and saluted him, he delivered to him,
with many thanks, the gold which he had promised;
and then falling at his feet, earnestly intreated, that he
might be made such as the Sorcerer himself was, pro-
mising that, if this could be effected through his means,
he would requite him with whatever sum he might

demand. But the Sorcerer replied, ' that it was not possible for him to be made a sorcerer also, because he was a Christian, having been made such by his baptism.' But Anthemius answered, ' then I renounce my baptism and Christian name, if I may be made a sorcerer.' Still the Sorcerer replied, ' thou canst not be made a sorcerer, neither canst thou keep the laws of the sorcerers, the which, if thou wert not to keep, thou wouldest then fall from a place which could never again be recovered.' But Anthemius, again embracing his feet, promised that he would perform whatever should be enjoined him: then the Sorcerer, seeing his perseverance, asked for paper, and having written therein what he thought good, gave it to Anthemius, and said, ' take this writing; and in the dead of the night go out of the city, supperless, and stand upon yonder little bridge. A huge multitude will pass over it about midnight, with a mighty uproar, and with their Prince seated in a chariot: yet fear not thou, for thou wilt not be hurt, having with thee this my writing; but hold up the writing, so that it may be perceived; and if thou shouldest be asked what thou doest there at that hour, or who thou art, say ' the Great Master sent me to my Lord the Prince, with this letter, that I might deliver it unto him.' But take heed neither to sign thyself as a Christian, nor to call upon Christ, for in either case thy desire would then be frustrated.'

" Anthemius therefore having received the letter, went

his way, and when night came he went out of the city,
and took his stand upon the little bridge, holding up the
writing in his hand. About midnight a great multitude
came there, and horsemen in great numbers, and the
Prince himself sitting in a chariot; and they who went
first surrounded him, saying, ' who is this that standeth
here?' To whom Anthemius made answer, ' the Great
Master hath sent me to my Lord the Prince with this
letter.' And they took the letter from him, and delivered it to the Prince who sate in the chariot, and he,
having received and read the same, wrote something in
the same paper, and gave it to Anthemius, that he should
carry it to the Sorcerer. So in the morning Anthemius,
having returned, delivered it to the Sorcerer, who, having perused it, said, ' wouldest thou know what he hath
written to us? even just as I before said to thee, to wit,
' knowest thou not that this man is a Christian? such a
one I can in no wise admit, unless, according to our
manner, he performeth all things, and renounceth and
abhorreth his faith.' When Anthemius heard this, he
replied, ' Master, now as elsewhile I abjure the name of
Christian, and the faith, and the baptism.' Then the
Sorcerer wrote again; and giving the writing to Anthemius, said, ' go again, and take thy stand at night at the
same place, and when he shall come, give him this, and
attend to what he shall say.' Accordingly he went his
way, and took his stand at the time and place appointed.
Behold at the same hour the same company appeared

again, and they said unto him, ' wherefore hast thou
returned hither?' Anthemius answered and said,
' Lord, the Great Master hath sent me back with this
writing.' The Prince then received it, and read, and
again wrote in it, and gave it again to be returned to the
Sorcerer. To whom Anthemius went again in the
morning, and he, having read the writing, said unto
him, ' knowest thou what he hath written unto me in
reply? I wrote to him, saying, ' all these things, Lord, he
hath abjured before me; admit him, therefore, if it
pleaseth thee.' But he hath written back, ' unless he
abjureth all this in writing, and in his own hand, I will
not admit him.' Say now, then, what wilt thou that I
should do for thee?'

" The wretched Anthemius answered and said,
' Master, I am ready to do this also.' And with that
he seated himself, and wrote thus.—I, Anthemius, abjure Christ and his faith. I abjure also his baptism, and
the cross, and the Christian name, and I promise that I
will never again use them, or invoke them. But, while
he was thus writing, a copious sweat ran from him, from
the top of his head to the soles of his feet, so that his
whole inner garment was wet therewith, as he himself
afterwards, with continual tears, confessed. He nevertheless went on writing, and, when it was finished, he
gave the writing to the Sorcerer to read, who, when he
had perused it, said, ' this is well; go thy way again,
and he will now certainly receive thee. And when he

shall have admitted thee, say to him reverently, I beseech thee, Lord, assign to me those who may be at my
bidding; and he will assign unto thee as many as thou
wilt have. But this I advise thee, not to take more than
one or two familiars, inasmuch as more would perplex
thee, and would be perpetually disturbing thee night and
day, that thou mightest give them what to do.' Then
Anthemius returned to the same place as before, and
awaited there, and the same company came there again
at midnight, and the leader of them, having incontinently
recognised Anthemius, began to cry out, ' Lord, the
Great Master hath again sent hither this man with his
commands:' and the Prince bade him draw nigh.
And Anthemius, drawing nigh, gave unto him his profession of abjuration, full of calamity and woe. He
having received and read it, raised it on high in his hand,
and began to exclaim, ' Christ, behold Anthemius, who
heretofore was thine, hath by this writing abjured and
execrated thee ! I am not the author of this his deed;
but he, offering himself to my service with many intrea-
ties, hath of his own accord written this his profession of
abjuration, and delivered it to me. Have thou then
therefore no care of him from this time forth!' And he
repeated these words a second time, and again a third.

" But when Anthemius heard that dreadful voice, he
trembled from head to foot, and began at the same time
to cry aloud, and to say, ' give me back the writing! I
am a Christian! I beseech thee, I adjure thee! I will be

a Christian! give me back the profession which I have
wickedly written!' But when the miserable man was
proceeding thus to exclaim, the Prince said unto him,
' never again mayest thou have this thy profession, which
I shall produce in the terrible day of judgement. From
this moment thou art mine, and I have thee in my
power at will, unless an outrage be done to justice.'
With these words he departed, leaving Anthemius.
But Anthemius lay prostrate on his face upon the bridge
till it was dawn, weeping and lamenting his condition.
As soon as it was daylight he rose and returned to his
own house, where he remained weeping and lamenting,
not knowing what he should do. Now there was another city, some eighteen miles off, where there was said
to be a Bishop, who was a man of God. To him, therefore, he resolved to repair, that he might obtain his
intercession, and having confessed the whole matter
even as it had taken place, to be again by him baptized:
for in his own city he was ashamed to confess what he
had done. Having then cut off his hair, and clad himself in sackcloth, he departed, and came unto that
Bishop, and having made himself known, was admitted
to him, and threw himself at his feet, saying, ' I beseech
thee, baptize me!' But the Bishop replied, ' can I believe that thou hast not yet been baptized?' Then he,
taking the Bishop apart, told him the whole matter, saying, ' I have indeed received baptism when I was a
child, but having now renounced in writing, behold I

am unbaptized!' To which the Bishop replied, 'how
camest thou persuaded that thou hast been unbaptized
of the baptism which thou hast received?' Anthemius
answered, ' in that unhappy hour when I wrote the
abjuration of my Lord and Saviour, and of his baptism,
incontinently a profuse sweat burst out, even from the
top of my head to the soles of my feet, so that my inner
garments were wet therewith; and from that time I
have believed of a truth, that even as I then abjured my
baptism, so did it depart from me. Now if thou canst,
O venerable Father, help me, in compassion upon one
who has thus voluntarily undone himself.' He said this
prostrate on the ground, and bedewed with tears.

   " When the man of God, the Bishop, heard this, he
threw himself upon the ground, and lay there beside
Anthemius, weeping and praying to the Lord. Then,
after a long while, rising, he roused Anthemius, and said
to him, ' verily, son, I dare not again purify by baptism
a man who hath been already baptized, for among
Christians there is no second baptism, except of tears.
Yet do not thou despair of thy salvation, nor of the
divine mercy, but rather commit thyself to God, praying
and humbly beseeching him for all the remainder of thy
life; and God, who is good and merciful, may render
back to thee the writing of thy abjuration, and moreover
forgive thee that impiety, as he forgave the ten thousand
talents to the debtor in the Gospel. Hope not to find a
better way than this, for there is no other to be found.'

He then being persuaded thus to do, and having obtained
the Bishop's prayers, went his way, weeping and groaning for the sin which he had committed; and having
returned home, he sold all his goods, and set at liberty
all his people, both men servants and maid servants,
giving them also of his possessions, and the rest of his
goods he distributed to the churches, and to the poor,
secretly, by the hand of a faithful servant. Moreover,
he gave three pounds of gold to the mother of that
Virgin, with the love of whom the Demon, to his own
destruction, had inflamed him, having placed them in a
certain church, saying, ' I beseech ye pray to God for
me a sinner: I shall never again trouble you, nor any
other person; for I depart I know not whither to bewail
the wickedness of my deeds.' Thus this man did,..and
from that time he was seen no more, casting himself
wholly upon the mercy of God, to which none who hath
betaken himself can perish.

" But we, who have heard the relation of this dreadful
thing, praise the Almighty Lord our God, and adore the
greatness of his works, that he hath protected the virgin
Maria in her holy intention of leading a single life, and
hath taken her mother out of poverty, affording liberally
to them both for their support and maintenance, and
hath delivered her also from the fear of sin, avoiding the
transgression of the oath, which had passed between
Maria the virgin and her enemy Anthemius, by annull-
ing it. For the Lord brought these things to pass before

the fifteen days, which were the appointed time between them, had elapsed. Wherefore we may say with the Evangelist, Our Lord hath done all things well. Nor hath he suffered the suppliant, who seeks him in penitence, to perish; for he saith, I came not to call the righteous, but sinners to repentance. Let us, therefore, continue to intreat him, that we may be protected by his Almighty hand, and may be delivered from all the devices of the Devil, and that, being aided by the prayers of the Saints, we may be worthy to attain the kingdom of Heaven. To the Lord our God belong all honour and glory and adoration, now and always, for ever and ever. Amen."

The Greeks appear to have delighted in fictions of this peculiar kind. The most extravagant of such legends is that of St. Justina and St. Cyprian, which Martene and Durand present as a veritable history, censuring Bishop Fell for treating it as fabulous! It is much too long for insertion in this place, but it would be injured by abridging it. The reader may find it in the *Thesaurus Novus Anecdotorum*, t. iii. pp. 1618—1650.

There on the everlasting ice
His dolorous throne was placed.—p. 18.

It was the north of Heaven that Lucifer, according to grave authors, attempted to take by storm. *En aver criado Dios con tanta hermosura el cielo y la tierra,*

quedo ordenada su celestial Corte de divinas Hierarchias ;
mas reynò tanto la ingratitud en uno de los Cortesanos,
viendose tan lindo y bello, y en mas eminente lugar que
los demas (segun Theodoreto) que quiso emparejar con el
Altissimo, y subir al Aquilon, formando para esto una
quadrilla de sus confidentes y parciales.

With this sentence Fr. Marco de Guadalajara y
Xavierr begins his account of the *Memorable Expulsion,*
y justissimo destierro de los Moriscos de España.

The marriage.—p. 42.

The description of the marriage service is taken from
Dr. King's work upon " the Rites and Ceremonies of
the Greek Church in Russia." " In all the offices of the
Greek Church," he says, " there is not perhaps a more
curious service than this of matrimony, nor any which
carries more genuine marks of antiquity; as from the
bare perusal of it may be seen, at one view, most of the
ceremonies which antiquarians have taken great pains
to ascertain." It agrees very closely with the ritual
given by Martene, *De Antiquis Ecclesiæ Ritibus,* t. ii.
pp. 390—8.

In these ceremonies,

" The which do endless matrimony make,"

the parties are betrothed to each other " for their salvation,".. " now and for ever, even unto ages of ages."

The Antenave.—p. 42.

The Προναος.

The coronals
Composed of all sweet flowers.—p. 46.

" Formerly these crowns were garlands made of
flowers or shrubs ; but now there are generally in all
churches crowns of silver, or other metals, kept for that
purpose."—*Dr. King's Rites, &c.* p. 232.

" A certain crown of flowers used in marriages," says
the excellent Bishop Heber, (writing from the Carnatic,)
" has been denounced to me as a device of Satan ! And
a gentleman has just written to complain that the Danish
Government of Tranquebar will not allow him to excommunicate some young persons for wearing masks,
and acting, as it appears, in a Christmas mummery, or
at least in some private rustic theatricals. If this be
heathenish, Heaven help the wicked ! But I hope you
will not suspect that I shall lend any countenance to this
kind of ecclesiastical tyranny, or consent to men's con-
sciences being burdened with restrictions so foreign to
the cheerful spirit of the Gospel."—vol. iii. pp. 446.

Basil, of living men
The powerfullest in prayer.—p. 71.

The most remarkable instance of St. Basil's power in
prayer is to be found, not in either of his lives, the vera-
cious or the apocryphal one, but in a very curious
account of the opinions held by the Armenian Christians,
as drawn up for the information of Pope Benedict XII.,
and inserted by Domenico Bernino in his *Historia di
tutte l'Heresie* (Secolo xiv. cap. iv. t. iii. pp. 508—536.)
It is there related that on the sixth day of the Creation,
when the rebellious angels fell from heaven through that
opening in' the firmament which the Armenians call
Arocea, and we the Galaxy, one unlucky angel, who had
no participation in their sin, but seems to have been
caught in the crowd, fell with them; and many others
would in like manner have fallen by no fault of their
own, if the Lord had not said unto them *Pax vobis.*
But this unfortunate angel was not restored till he
obtained, it is not said how, the prayers of St. Basil; his
condition meantime, from the sixth day of the Creation
to the fourth century of the Christian era, must have
been even more uncomfortable than that of Klopstock's
repentant Devil.—p. 512, § 16.

Eleëmon's penance.—p. 72.

In the legend the penitent is left forty days and nights to contend with the Powers of Darkness in the Relic Chamber.

Captain Hall relates an amusing example of the manner in which penance may be managed at this time in Mexico.

" I went," he says, " to the Convent of La Cruz to visit a friend who was doing penance, not for a sin he had committed, but for one he was preparing to commit. The case was this:.. Don N. had recently lost his wife, and, not choosing to live in solitude, looked about for another helpmate; and being of a disposition to take little trouble in such a research, or, probably, thinking that no labour could procure for him any one so suitable as what his own house afforded, he proposed the matter to his lately lamented wife's sister, who had lived in his house several years; and who, as he told me himself, was not only a very good sort of person, but one well acquainted with all the details of his household, known and esteemed by his children, and accustomed to his society.

" The church, however, looked exceedingly grave upon the occasion; not, however, as I at first supposed, from the nearness of the connection, or the shortness of the interval since the first wife's death, but because the intended lady had stood godmother to four of Don N.'s children. This, the church said, was a serious bar to

K

the new alliance, which nothing could surmount but protracted penances and extensive charity. Don N. was urgent; and a council was assembled to deliberate on the matter. The learned body declared, after some discussion, the case to be a very knotty one; and that, as the lady had been four times godmother to Don N.'s children, it was impossible she could marry him. Nevertheless, the Fathers (compassionate persons!) wished to give the unhappy couple another chance; and agreed to refer the question to a learned doctor in the neighbourhood, skilled in all difficult questions of casuistry. This sage person decided that, according to the canons of the church, the marriage might take place, on payment of a fine of four hundred dollars: two for the poor in pocket, and two for the poor in spirit; namely, the priests. But, to expiate the crime of marrying a quadruple godmother, a slight penance must also be submitted to in the following manner. Don N. was to place himself on his knees before the altar, with a long wax candle burning in his hand, while his intended lady stood by his side, holding another: this was to be repeated in the face of the congregation, for one hour, during every Sunday and fast-day throughout a whole year; after which purifying exposure, the parties were to be held eligible to proceed with the marriage. Don N., who chose rather to put his conscience than his knees to such discipline, took his own measures on the occasion. What these were, the idle public took the

liberty of guessing broadly enough, but no one could say
positively. At the end of a week, however, it was
announced, that the case had undergone a careful re-ex-
amination, and that it had been deemed proper to com-
mute the penance into one week's retirement from the
world: that is to say, Don N. was to shut himself up in
the Convent of La Cruz, there to fast and pray in solitude and silence for seven days. The manner in which
this penance was performed is an appropriate commentary
on the whole transaction. The penitent, aided and
assisted by two or three of the jovial friars of the convent, passed the evening in discussing some capital
wine, sent out for the occasion by Don N. himself, after
eating a dinner, prepared by the cook of the convent,
the best in New Galicia. As for silence and solitude,
his romping boys and girls were with him during all the
morning; besides a score of visitors, who strolled daily
out of town as far as the convent, to keep up the poor
man's spirits, by relating all the gossip which was afloat
about his marriage, his penitence, and the wonderful
kindness of the church."—*Capt. Hall's Journal*, vol. ii.
pp. 210—214.

" I have read of a gentleman," says Bishop Taylor,
" who, being on his death-bed, and his confessor search-
ing and dressing of his wounded soul, was found to be
obliged to make restitution of a considerable sum of
money, with the diminution of his estate. His confessor
found him desirous to be saved, a lover of his religion,

and yet to have a kindness for his estate, which he
desired might be entirely transmitted to his beloved
heir: he would serve God with all his heart, and
repented him of his sin, of his rapine and injustice; he
begged for pardon passionately, he humbly hoped for
mercy, he resolved, in case he did recover, to live
strictly, to love God, to reverence his priests, to be
charitable to the poor; but to make restitution he found
impossible to him, and he hoped the commandment
would not require it of him, and desired to be relieved
by an easy and a favourable interpretation; for it is ten
thousand pities so many good actions and good purposes
should be in vain, but it is worse, infinitely worse, if the
man should perish. What should the confessor do in
this case?—shall not the man be relieved, and his piety
be accepted; or shall the rigour and severity of his confessor, and his scrupulous fears and impertinent niceness,
cast away a soul either into future misery, or present
discomfort? neither one nor other was to be done; and
the good man was only to consider what God had made
necessary, not what the vices of his penitent and his
present follies should make so. Well: the priest insists
upon his first resolution, ' Non dimittitur peccatum, nisi
restituatur ablatum:' the sick man could have no ease
by the loss of a duty. The poor clinic desires the confessor to deal with his son, and try if he could be made
willing that his father might go to heaven at the charge
of his son, which when he had attempted, he was

answered with extreme rudeness and injurious language; which caused great trouble to the priest and to the dying father. At last the religious man found out this device, telling his penitent, that unless by corporal penances there could be made satisfaction in exchange of restitution, he knew no hopes; but because the profit of the estate, which was obliged to restitution, was to descend upon the son, he thought something might be hoped, if, by way of commutation, the son would hold his finger in a burning candle for a quarter of an hour. The glad father being overjoyed at this loop-hole of eternity, this glimpse of heaven, and the certain retaining of the whole estate, called to his son, told him the condition and the advantages to them both, making no question but he would gladly undertake the penance. But the son with indignation replied, ' he would not endure so much torture to save the whole estate.' To which the priest, espying his advantage, made this quick return to the old man : ' Sir, if your son will not, for a quarter of an hour, endure the pains of a burning finger to save your soul, will you, to save a portion of the estate for him, endure the flames of hell to eternal ages ?' The unreasonableness of the odds, and the ungratefulness of the son, and the importunity of the priest, and the fear of hell, and the indispensable necessity of restitution, awakened the old man from his lethargy, and he bowed himself to the rule, made restitution, and had hopes of pardon and present comfort."—*Works of Jeremy Taylor*, vol. xiii. p. 38.

The penances which Indian fanatics voluntarily undertake and perform would be deemed impossible in Europe, if they had not been witnessed by so many persons of unquestionable authority. The penances which the Bramins enjoin are probably more severe than they would otherwise be, on this account, lest they should seem trifling in the eyes of a people accustomed to such exhibitions.

" If a Shoodru go to a Bramhunee of bad character, he must renounce life by casting himself into a large fire. If a Shoodru go to a Bramhunee of unsullied character, he must tie straw round the different parts of his body, and cast himself into the fire. The woman must be placed on an ass and led round the city, and then *go the Great Way* : the meaning of this is, she must wander to those sacred places of the Hindoos where the climate is exceedingly cold, and proceed till she actually perish with cold. This is a meritorious way of terminating life, and is mentioned as such in the Hindoo writings." —*Ward*, vol. i. p. 427.

Sometimes the law is frustrated by its own severity. " It is a dogma of general notoriety, that if a Jungum has the mischance to lose his Lingum, he ought not to survive the misfortune. Poornia, the present minister of Mysoor, relates an incident of a Ling-ayet friend of

his, who had unhappily lost his portable god, and came
to take a last farewell. The Indians, like more enlight-
ened nations, readily laugh at the absurdities of every
sect but their own, and Poornia gave him better counsel.
It is a part of the ceremonial, preceding the sacrifice of
the individual, that the principal persons of the sect
should assemble on the banks of some holy stream, and
placing in a basket the lingum images of the whole
assembly, purify them in the sacred waters. The des-
tined victim, in conformity to the advice of his friend,
suddenly seized the basket, and overturned its contents
into the rapid Caveri. ‘ Now, my friends,’ said he, ‘ we
are on equal terms : let us prepare to die together.’
The discussion terminated according to expectation.
The whole party took an oath of inviolable secresy, and
each privately provided himself with a new image of the
lingum.”— *Wilks*, vol. i. p. 506.

In 1790, when the Mahrattas were to have co-ope-
rated with Lord Cornwallis at Seringapatam, their
general, Parasu Ram Bhao, became unclean from eating
with a Bramin who had — kissed a cobler's wife.
There was no stream near holy enough to wash away
the impurity, so he marched his whole immense army
to the junction of the Tungha and the Badra. Major
Moor, who was with him, says, “ during this march,
uncalled for in a military point of view, the army laid
waste scores of towns and thousands of acres, .. indeed,
whole districts; we fought battles, stormed forts, destroyed

a large army, and ran every military risk. Having
reached the sacred place of junction, he washed, and
having been made clean, was weighed against gold and
silver; his weight was 16,000 pagodas, about £7000,
which was given to the Bramins. They who had eaten
with the Bramin at the same time, in like manner
washed away the defilement; but the weighing is a ceremony peculiar to the great."—*Moor's Hindu Infanticide,*
p. 234.

" The present king of Travancore has conquered, or
carried war into all the countries which lay round his
dominions, and lives in the continual exercise of his
arms. To atone for the blood which he has spilt, the
Brachmans persuaded him that it was necessary he
should be born anew : this ceremony consisted in putting
the prince into the body of a golden cow of immense
value, where, after he had lain the time prescribed; he
came out regenerated, and freed from all the crimes of
his former life. The cow was afterwards cut up, and
divided amongst the seers who had invented this extra-
ordinary method for the remission of his sins."—*Orme's
Fragments.*

. A far less expensive form was observed among the
ancient Greeks, in cases wherein a second birth was
deemed indispensable, " for in Greece they thought not
those pure and clean who had been carried forth for
dead to be interred, or whose sepulchre and funerals had
been solemnized or prepared; neither were such allowed

to frequent the company of others, nor suffered to come
near unto their sacrifices.   And there goeth a report of
a certain man named Aristinus, one of those who had
been possessed with this superstition; how he sent unto
the oracle of Apollo at Delphos, for to make supplication
and prayer unto the god, for to be delivered out of this
perplexed anxiety that troubled him by occasion of the
said custom, or law, then in force, and that the pro-
phetess Pythia returned this answer :

> " Look whatsoever women do,
>   in childbed newly laid,
> Unto their babes which they brought forth,
>   the very same, I say,   .
> See that be done to thee again ;
>   and after that, be sure,
> Unto the blessed Gods with hands
>   to sacrifice, most pure.

" Which oracle thus delivered, Aristinus, having well
pondered and considered, committed himself as an infant
new born unto women, for to be washed, to be wrapped
in swaddling clothes, and to be suckled with the breast-
head : after which all such others, whom we call *Hyste-
ropotmous*, that is to say, those whose graves were made
as if they were dead, did the semblable.   Howbeit some
do say that, before Aristinus was born, these ceremonies
were observed about these Hysteropotmoi, and that this
was a right ancient custom kept in the semblable case."
—*Plutarch's Morals, tr. by Philemon Holland*, p. 852.

The lamps went out.—p. 78.

There is the authority of a Holy Man in the Romance of Merlin,.. which is as good authority for such a fact as anything in the Acta Sanctorum,.. that the Devil, like other wild beasts who prowl about seeking what they may devour, is afraid of a light. The Holy Man's advice to a pious damsel is never to lie down in the dark; " *garde que la ou tu coucheras il y ait tousjours clarté, car le Diable hait toutes cleres choses; ne ne vient pas voulentiers ou il y a clarte.*"—vol. i. ff. 4.

And white is black, and black is white.—p. 100.

Satan might have been reconciled to St. Basil's profession if he had understood, by his faculty of second-sight, that this, which it is sometimes the business of a lawyer to prove, would one day be the duty of the Roman Catholics to *believe*, if their church were to tell them so. No less a personage than St. Ignatius Loyola has asserted this. In his *Exercitia Spiritualia*, the 13th of the Rules which are laid down *ad sentiendum cum Ecclesiá*, is in these words :

" *Denique, ut ipsi Ecclesiæ Catholicæ omnino unanimes, conformesque simus*, si quid, quod oculis nostris apparet album, nigrum illa esse definierit, debemus itidem, quod nigrum sit, pronuntiare. *Indubitate nam-*

que credendum est, eumdem esse Domini nostri Jesu Christi, et Ecclesiæ orthodoxæ, sponsæ ejus, spiritum, per quem gubernamur ac dirigimur ad salutem ; neque alium esse Deum, qui olim tradidit Decalogi præcepta, et qui nunc temporis Ecclesiam hierarchicam instruit atque regit."—p. 141, Antwerpiæ, 1635

Such is the implicit obedience enjoined in those Spiritual Exercises, of which Pope Paul III. said in his brief, *sub annulo Piscatoris,* " *omnia et singula in eis contenta, ex certâ scientiâ nostrâ, approbamus, collaudamus, ac præsentis scripti patrocinio communimus.*" The Roman Catholics are to believe that black is white if the Roman Church tells them so: morally and politically it has often told them so, and *they have believed and acted accordingly.*

The impious scroll was dropt, a blank,
At Eleëmon's feet.—p. 104.

This is not the only miracle of this kind recorded of St. Basil.

" There was a certain woman of noble family, and born of rich parents, who was wholly made up of the vanities of this world, and beyond measure arrogant in all things; she, becoming a widow, wasted her substance shamelessly, living a loose and profligate life, doing none of those things which are enjoined by the Lord, but wallowing like a swine in the mire and filth of her iniquities. But being at length by the will of God brought to a consideration of her own estate, and her mind filled with consciousness of the immeasurable offences which she had committed, she called to remembrance the multitude of her sins, and bewailed them penitently, saying, ' Woe to me a sinner, how shall I render an account of the multitude of my sins! I have profaned a spiritual temple; I have defiled the soul which inhabiteth this body! Woe is me, woe is me! what have I done! what hath befallen me! Shall I say, like the Harlot or the Publican, that I have sinned? But no one has sinned like me! How, then, shall I be assured that God will receive my repentance?' While she meditated in herself upon these things, He, who would that all should be saved and brought back into the way of truth, and would have no one perish, was pleased to bring unto her remembrance all the sins which she had committed from her youth up. And she set down in writing all these offences, even all that she had committed from her youth to this her elder age; and, last of all, she set down one great and heinous sin, the worst of all; and having done this, she folded up the writing, and fastened it with lead. After this, having waited till a convenient season, when holy Basil was accustomed to go to the church that he might pray there, she ran before to meet him, and threw the writing at his feet, and prostrated herself before

him, saying, ' O, holy man of God, have compassion
upon me a sinner, yea, the vilest of sinners !' The most
blessed man stopt thereat, and asked of her ' wherefore
she thus groaned and lamented :' and she said unto him,
' Saint of God, see I have set down all my sins and iniquities in this writing, and I have folded it, and fastened
it with lead ; do not thou, I charge thee, open it, but by
thy powerful prayers blot out all that is written therein.'
Then the great and holy Basil held up the writing, and,
looking toward Heaven, said, ' O Lord, to Thee alone
all the deeds of this woman are manifest! Thou hast
taken away the sins of the world, and more easily mayest
thou blot out those of this single soul. Before thee,
indeed, all our offences are numbered; but thy mercy is
infinite.' Saying thus, he went into the church, holding
the aforesaid writing in his hand; and prostrating himself before the altar, there he remained through the
night, and on the morrow, during the performance of all
the masses which were celebrated there, intreating God
for this woman's sake. And when she came to him, he
gave her the writing, and said to her, ' Woman, hast
thou heard that the remission of sins can come from
God alone ?' She answered, ' Yea, father; and therefore have I supplicated thee that thou shouldst intercede
with that most merciful God in my behalf.' And then
she opened the writing, and found that it was all blotted
out, save only that the one great, and most heinous sin,
still remained written there. But she, seeing that this

great sin was still legible as before, beat her breast, and
began to bewail herself, and falling at his feet again,
with many tears she said, ' have compassion upon me,
O Servant of the Most High, and as thou hast once
exerted thyself in prayer for all my sins, and hast prevailed, so now intercede, as thou canst, that this offence
also may be blotted out.' Thereat holy Basil wept for
pity; and he said unto her, ' Woman arise! I also am
a sinner, and have myself need of forgiveness: He who
hath blotted out thus much, hath granted thee remission
of thy sins as far as hath to Him seemed good; and
God, who hath taken away the sins of the world, is able
to take from thee this remaining sin also; and if thou
wilt keep his commandments, and walk in his ways, thou
shalt not only have forgiveness, but wilt also become
worthy of glory. But go thou into the desert, and there
thou wilt find a holy man, who is well known to all the
holy fathers, and who is called Ephræm. Give thou
this writing to him, and he will intercede for thee, and
will prevail with the Lord.'

" The woman then commended herself to the holy
Bishop's prayers, and hastened away into the desert, and
performed a long journey therein. She came to the
great and wonderful Hermit, who was called Ephræm
by name, and knocking at his door, she cried aloud, saying, ' have compassion on me, saint of God, have compassion on me !' But he, having been forewarned in
spirit concerning the errand on which she came, replied

unto her, saying, ' Woman depart, for I also am a man
and a sinner, standing myself in need of an intercessor.'
But she held out the writing, and said, ' the holy Archbishop Basil sent me to thee, that thou mightest intercede for me, and that therethrough the sin which is
written herein might be blotted out. The other many
sins holy Basil hath blotted out by his prayers : Saint of
God, do not thou think it much to intercede with the
Lord for me for this one sin, seeing that I am sent unto
thee to that end.' But that confessor made answer,
' No, daughter ! Could he obtain from the Lord the
remission of so many other sins, and cannot he intercede
and prevail for this single one? Go thy way back,
therefore, and tarry not, that thou mayest find him
before his soul be departed from his body.' Then the
woman commended herself to the holy Confessor
Ephræm, and returned to Cæsarea.

" But, when she entered that city, she met the persons
who were bearing the body of St. Basil to burial ; seeing
which, she threw herself upon the ground, and began to
cry aloud against the holy man, saying, ' Woe is me a
sinner, woe is me a lost wretch, woe is me ! O man of
God thou hast sent me into the desert, that thou
mightest be rid of me, and not wearied more; and
behold I am returned from my bootless journey, having
gone over so great a way in vain ! The Lord God see
to this thing, and judge between me and thee, inasmuch
as thou couldest have interceded with Him for me, and

have prevailed, if thou hadst not sent me away to another.' Saying this, she threw the writing upon the bier
whereon the body of holy Basil was borne, and related
before the people all that past between them. One of
the clergy then desiring to know what this one sin was,
took up the writing, and opened it, and found that it was
clean blotted out: whereupon he cried with a loud voice
unto the woman, and said, ' O woman, there is nothing
written herein! Why dost thou consume thyself with
so much labour and sorrow, not knowing the great things
of God unto thee ward, and his inscrutable mercies?'
Then the multitude of the people, seeing this glorious
and great miracle, glorified God, who hath such power,
that he remitteth the sins of all who are living, and
giveth grace to his servants, that after their decease they
should heal all sickness and all infirmity: and hath
given unto them power for remitting all sins to those
who preserve a right faith in the Lord, continuing in
good works, and glorifying God and our Lord and
Saviour."—*Vitæ Patrum*, pp. 159, 160.

" In the days of the blessed Theodemir, Bishop of
Compostella, there was a certain Italian, who had hardly
dared confess to his own Priest and Bishop a certain
enormous crime which he had formerly committed. His
Bishop having heard the confession, and being struck
with astonishment and horror at so great an offence,
dared not appoint what penance he should perform.
Nevertheless, being moved with compassion, he sent the

sinner with a schedule, in which the offence was written, to the Church of Santiago at Compostella, enjoining him that he should, with his whole heart, implore the aid of the blessed Apostle, and submit himself to the sentence of the Bishop of that Apostolical Church. He therefore without delay went to Santiago in Galicia, and there placed the schedule, which contained the statement of his crime, upon the venerable altar, repenting that he had committed so great a sin, and intreating forgiveness, with tears and sobs, from God and the Apostle. This was on Santiago's Day, being the eighth of the Kalends of August, and at the first hour.

" When the blessed Theodemir, Bishop of the See of Compostella, came attired in his pontificals to sing mass at the altar that day at the third hour, he found the schedule under the covering of the altar, and demanded forthwith, wherefore, and by whom it had been placed there. The Penitent upon this came forward, and on his knees declared, with many tears, before all the people, the crime which he had committed, and the injunctions which had been laid on him by his own Bishop. The holy Bishop then opened the schedule, and found nothing written therein; it appeared as if no letters had ever been inscribed there. A marvellous thing, and an exceeding joy, for which great praise and glory were incontinently rendered to God and the Apostle, the people all singing, ' this is the Lord's doing, and it is marvellous in our eyes!' The holy Bishop then

L

of a truth believing, that the penitent had obtained forgiveness with God through the merits of the Apostle, would impose upon him no other penance for the crime which he had committed, except that of keeping Friday as a fast from that time forth, and having absolved him from all his other sins, he dismissed him to his own country. Hence it may be inferred, that if any one shall truly repent, and, going from distant countries to Galicia, shall there, with his whole heart, intreat pardon from God, and pray for the aid of the blessed Santiago, the record of his misdeeds shall, without all doubt, be blotted out for ever."—*Acta SS.* Jul. t. vi. p. 48.

There is a miracle of the same kind related of St. Antonio, .. and probably many other examples might be found.

END OF ALL FOR LOVE.

THE

PILGRIM TO COMPOSTELLA:

BEING

THE LEGEND OF A COCK AND A HEN,

TO

THE HONOUR AND GLORY

OF

SANTIAGO.

—————

A CHRISTMAS TALE.

—————

" Res similis ficta ; sed quid mihi fingere prodest."
Ovid, Met. xiii. v. 935
" Hear also no lean story of theirs !"
Lightfoot.

THE Legend, (for a genuine Legend it is,) which has
been made the subject of the ensuing Ballad, is related
by Bishop Patrick in his Parable of the Pilgrim.
(ch. xxxv. pp. 430—434.) Udal ap Rhys relates it in
his Tour through Spain and Portugal. (pp. 35—38.)
Both these writers refer to Lucius Marineus Siculus as
their authority. And it is told also in the *Journal du
Voyage d'Espagne*, (Paris, 1669,) by a *Conseiller* who
was attached to the French Embassy in that country.
(p. 18.)

The story may likewise be found in the *Acta Sanctorum*. A duplicate of the principal miracle occurs in the
third volume, for the month of May, (*die* 12ᵃ, p. 171,)
and is there ascribed to S. Domingo de la Calzada, the
author, Luiz de la Vega, contending, that both relations
are to be received as true, the Bollandist (Henschenius)
contrariwise opining that they are distinct miracles, but
leaving the reader nevertheless to determine freely for
himself *utrum id malit, an vero credere velit, unicum
dumtaxat esse quod sub quadam circumstantiarum varie-
tate refertur ut geminum.*

In the sixth volume of the same work, for the month
of July, (*die* 25ᵃ,) the legend of the Pilgrim is twice
told, once (p. 45) as occurring to a native of Utrecht,
(Cæsarius Heisterbachensis is the authority,) once as
having befallen a German at Thoulouse (p. 50); the
latter story is in the collection of Santiago's miracles,

which Pope Calixtus II. is said to have compiled. The extract from Lucius Marineus Siculus may also be seen there. It is here annexed as it stands in the fifth book of that author's work *de rebus Hispaniæ memorabilibus.*

" *In antiquissimâ civitate quam Sancti Dominici Calciatensis, vulgus appellat, gallum vidimus et gallinam, qui dum vixerunt, cujus coloris fuissent ignoramus : postea vero cum jugulati fuissent et assi, candidissimi revixerunt, magnam Dei potentiam summumque miraculum referentes. Cujus rei veritas et ratio sic se habet. Vir quidam probus et amicus Dei, et uxor ejus, optima mulier, cum filio adolescentulo magnæ probitatis, ad Sanctum Jacobum Compostellam proficiscentes, in hanc urbem itineris labore defessi ingrediuntur, et quiescendi gratiâ restiterunt in domo cujusdam qui adultam filiam habebat. Quæ cum adolescentem pulchrâ facie vidisset, ejus amore capta est. Et cum juvenis ab ea requisitus atque vexatus, ejus voto repugnasset, amorem convertit in odium, et ei nocere cupiens, tempore quo discedere volebant ejus cucullo crateram sui patris clam reposuit. Cumque peregrini mane discessissent, exclamavit puella coram parentibus crateram sibi fuisse subreptam. Quod audiens Prætor satellites confestim misit, ut peregrinos reducerent. Qui cum venissent, puella conscia sui sceleris accessit ad juvenem et crateram eruit e cucullo. Quapropter comperto delicto, juvenis in campum productus iniquâ sententiâ et sine culpâ laqueo suspensus est : miserique parentes cum filium deplorassent, postea discedentes*

Compostellam pervenerunt. Ubi solutis votis et Deo gratias agentes subinde redeuntes ad locum pervenerunt, ubi filius erat suspensus, et mater multis perfusa lacrymis ad filium accessit, multùm desuadente marito. Cumque filium suspiceret, dixit ei filius, Mater mea noli flere super me: ego enim vivus sum, quoniam Virgo Dei genetrix, et Sanctus Jacobus me sustinent et servant incolumem. Vade charissima mater ad judicem qui me falsò condemnavit, et dic ei me vivere propter innocentiam meam, ut me liberari jubeat, tibique restituat. Properat solicita mater, et præ nimio gaudio flens uberius, Prætorem convenit in mensâ sedentem, qui gallum et gallinam assos scindere volebat. ' Prætor, inquit, filius meus vivit ; jube solvi, obsecro !' Quod cum audisset Prætor, existimans eam quod dicebat propter amorem maternum somniasse, respondit subridens, ' quid hoc est, bona mulier ? Ne fallaris! sic enim vivit filius tuus, ut vivunt hæ aves !' Et vix hoc dixerat cum gallus et gallina saltaverunt in mensâ, statimque gallus cantavit. Quod cum Prætor vidisset attonitus continuo egreditur, vocat sacerdotes, et cives, proficiscuntur ad juvenem suspensum : et invenerunt incolumem valdeque lætantem, et parentibus restituunt ; domumque reversi gallum capiunt et gallinam, et in ecclesiam transferunt magnâ solemnitate. Quæ ibi clausæ res admirabiles et Dei potentiam testificantes observantur, ubi septennio vivunt ; hunc enim terminum Deus illis instituit ; et in fine septennii antequam moriantur, pullum relinquunt et pullam sui coloris et

magnitudinis ; et hoc fit in eâ ecclesiâ quolibet septennio.
Magnæ quoque admirationis est, quod omnes per hanc
urbem transeuntes peregrini, qui sunt innumerabiles, galli
hujus et gallinæ plumam capiunt, et numquam illis plumæ
deficiunt. Hoc ego testor, propterea quod vidi et inter-
.fui, plumamque mecum fero."—Rerum Hispanicarum
Scriptores, t. ii. p. 805.

Luiz de la Vega agrees with Marineus Siculus in all
the particulars of this perpetual miracle, except the latter;
" *sed scriptorem illum fictionis arguit, quod asserat,*
plumas galli et gallinæ, quæ quotidie peregrinis illac
transeuntibus distribuuntur, prodigiose multiplicari : af-
firmat autem tamquam testis oculatus, in eâ ecclesiâ
designatum esse quemdam clericum, qui plumas illas con-
servit et peregrinis distribuit ; at negat continuum mul-
tiplicationis miraculum à Marineo Siculo tam confidenter
assertum, in eâ urbe videri, aut patrari. Multis tamen
probare nititur, reliqua omnia prodigia esse vera, testatur-
que ad perpetuam rei memoriam in superiori ecclesiæ
parte omnium oculis exponi idem patibulum, in quo
peregrinus suspensus fuit."—Acta Sanctorum, Jul. t. vi.
p. 46.

THE PILGRIM TO COMPOSTELLA.

PRELUDE.

" TELL us a story, old Robin Gray!
This merry Christmas time :
We are all in our glory, so tell us a story,
   Either in prose, or in rhyme.

" Open your budget, old Robin Gray!
   We very well know it is full :
Come ! out with a murder,.. a Goblin,.. a Ghost,
   Or a tale of a Cock and a Bull!"

" I have no tale of a Cock and a Bull,
   My good little women and men ;
But 'twill do as well, perhaps, if I tell
   A tale of a Cock and a Hen."

INTRODUCTION.

You have all of you heard of St. James for Spain,
    As one of the Champions Seven,
Who, having been good Knights on Earth,
    Became Hermits and Saints in Heaven.

Their history once was in good repute,
    And so it ought to be still;
Little friends, I dare say you have read it:
    And if not, why I hope you will.

Of this St. James that book proclaims
    Great actions manifold:
But more amazing are the things
    Which of him in Spain are told.

How once a ship, of marble made,
Came sailing o'er the sea,
Wherein his headless corpse was laid,
Perfumed with sanctity.

And how, tho' then he had no head,
He afterwards had two;
Which both worked miracles so well,
That it was not possible to tell
The false one from the true.*

---

* Whereby my little friends, we see
That an original may sometimes be
No better than its fac-simile;
A useful truth I trow,
Which picture buyers won't believe,
But which picture dealers know.

Young Connoisseurs who will be!
Remember I say this,..
For your benefit hereafter,..
In a parenthesis.

And not to interrupt
The order of narration,
This warning shall be printed
By way of annotation.

And how he used to fight the Moors
 Upon a milk-white charger:
Large tales of him the Spaniards tell,
 Munchausen tells no larger.

But in their cause of latter years
 He has not been so hearty:
For that he never struck a stroke is plain,
When our Duke, in many a hard campaign,
Beat the French armies out of Spain,
 And conquered Buonaparte.

Yet still they worship him in Spain,
And believe in him with might and main:
 Santiago there they call him:
And if any one there should doubt these tales,
 They've an Inquisition to maul him.

At Compostella in his Church

His body and one head
Have been for some eight hundred years
By Pilgrims visited.

Old scores might there be clean rubb'd off,
And tickets there were given
To clear all toll gates on the way
Between the Churchyard and Heaven.

Some went for payment of a vow
In time of trouble made;
And some who found that pilgrimage
Was a pleasant sort of trade.

And some, I trow, because it was
Believed, as well as said,
That all, who in their mortal stage
Did not perform this pilgrimage,
Must make it when they were dead.

Some upon penance for their sins,
In person, or by attorney:
And some who were, or had been sick;
And some who thought to cheat Old Nick;
And some who liked the journey:

Which well they might when ways were safe;
And therefore rich and poor
Went in that age on pilgrimage,
As folks now make a tour.

The poor with scrip, the rich with purse,
They took their chance for better for worse
From many a foreign land,
With a scallop-shell in the hat for badge,
And a Pilgrim's staff in hand.

Something there is, the which to leave
Untold would not be well,

Relating to the Pilgrim's staff,
And to the scallop-shell.

For the scallop shows in a coat of arms,
That of the bearer's line
Some one, in former days, hath been
To Santiago's shrine.

And the staff was bored and holed for those
Who on a flute could play,
And thus the merry Pilgrim had
His music on the way.

THE LEGEND.

PART I.

ONCE on a time three Pilgrims true,
Being Father and Mother and Son,
For pure devotion to the Saint,
This pilgrimage begun.

Their names, little friends, I am sorry to say,
In none of my books can I find;
But the son, if you please, we'll call Pierre,
What the parents were called, never mind.

From France they came, in which fair land
They were people of good renown;
And they took up their lodging one night on the way
In La Calzada town.

Now, if poor Pilgrims they had been,
And had lodged in the Hospice instead of the Inn,
My good little women and men,
Why then you never would have heard,
This tale of the Cock and the Hen!

For the Innkeepers they had a daughter,
Sad to say, who was just such another
As Potiphar's daughter, I think, would have been
If she followed the ways of her mother.

This wicked woman to our Pierre
Behaved like Potiphar's wife;
And, because she fail'd to win his love,
She resolved to take his life.

So she pack'd up a silver cup
In his wallet privily:
And then, as soon as they were gone,
She raised a hue and cry.

M

The Pilgrims were overtaken:
The people gathered round.
Their wallets were search'd, and in Pierre's
The silver cup was found.

They dragg'd him before the Alcayde;
A hasty Judge was he:
" The theft," he said, " was plain and proved,
And hang'd the thief must be."
So to the gallows our poor Pierre
Was hurried instantly.

If I should now relate
The piteous lamentation,
Which for their son these parents made,
My little friends, I am afraid
You'd weep at the relation.

But Pierre in Santiago still

His constant faith profess'd;
When to the gallows he was led,
" 'Twas a short way to Heaven," he said;
" Tho' not the pleasantest."

And from their pilgrimage he charged
His parents not to cease,
Saying that unless they promised this,
He could not be hang'd in peace.

They promised it with heavy hearts;
Pierre then; therewith content,
Was hang'd: and they upon their way
To Compostella went.

PART II.

FOUR weeks they travelled painfully,
They paid their vows, and then
To La Calzada's fatal town
Did they come back again.

The Mother would not be withheld,
But go she must to see
Where her poor Pierre was left to hang
Upon the gallows tree.

Oh tale most marvellous to hear,
Most marvellous to tell!
Eight weeks had he been hanging there,
And yet was alive and well!

" Mother," said he, " I am glad you're return'd,
    It is time I should now be releas'd :
Tho' I cannot complain that I'm tired,
    And my neck does not ache in the least.

" The Sun has not scorch'd me by day,
    The Moon has not chilled me by night;
And the winds have but help'd me to swing,
    As if in a dream of delight.

" Go you to the Alcayde,
    That hasty Judge unjust:
Tell him Santiago has saved me,
    And take me down he must !"

Now, you must know the Alcayde,
    Not thinking himself a great sinner,
Just then at table had sate down,
    About to begin his dinner.

His knife was raised to carve,
The dish before him then:
Two roasted fowls were laid therein;
That very morning they had been
A Cock and his faithful Hen.

In came the Mother wild with joy;
" A miracle !" she cried;
But that most hasty Judge unjust
Repell'd her in his pride.

" Think not," quoth he, " to tales like this
That I should give belief!
Santiago never would bestow
His miracles, full well I know,
On a Frenchman and a thief."

And pointing to the Fowls, o'er which
He held his ready knife,

" As easily might I believe
These birds should come to life!"

The good Saint would not let him thus
The Mother's true tale withstand;
So up rose the Fowls in the dish,
And down dropt the knife from his hand.

The Cock would have crowed if he could;
To cackle the Hen had a wish;
And they both slipt about in the gravy
Before they got out of the dish.

And when each would have open'd its eyes,
For the purpose of looking about them,
They saw they had no eyes to open,
And that there was no seeing without them.

All this was to them a great wonder;

They stagger'd and reel'd on the table;
And either to guess where they were,
Or what was their plight, or how they came there,
Alas! they were wholly unable:

Because, you must know, that that morning,
A thing which they thought very hard,
The Cook had cut off their heads,
And thrown them away in the yard.

The Hen would have prank'd up her feathers,
But plucking had sadly deformed her;
And for want of them she would have shivered with cold,
If the roasting she had had had not warm'd her.

And the Cock felt exceedingly queer;
He thought it a very odd thing
That his head and his voice were he did not know where,
And his gizzard tuck'd under his wing.

The gizzard got into its place,
But how Santiago knows best:
And so, by the help of the Saint,
Did the liver and all the rest.

The heads saw their way to the bodies,
In they came from the yard without check,
And each took its own proper station,
To the very great joy of the neck.

And in flew the feathers, like snow in a shower,
For they all became white on the way;
And the Cock and the Hen in a trice were refledged,
And then who so happy as they!

Cluck! cluck! cried the Hen right merrily then,
The Cock his clarion blew,
Full glad was he to hear again
His own cock-a-doo-del-doo!

PART III.

" A Miracle ! a miracle !"
The people shouted, as they might well,
When the news went thro' the town ;
And every child and woman and man
Took up the cry, and away they ran
To see Pierre taken down.

They made a famous procession ;
My good little women and men,
Such a sight was never seen before,
And I think will never again.

Santiago's Image, large as life,
Went first with banners and drum and fife,
And next, as was most meet,

The twice-born Cock and Hen were borne
  Along the thronging street.

Perch'd on a cross-pole hoisted high,
They were raised in sight óf the crowd;
And, when the people set up a cry,
The Hen she-cluck'd in sympathy,
  And the Cock he crow'd aloud.

And because they very well knew for why
They were carried in such solemnity,
And saw the Saint and his banners before 'em,
They behaved with the greatest propriety,
  And most correct decorum.

The Knife, which had cut off their heads that morn,
  Still red with their innocent blood, was borne,
    The scullion boy he carried it;
And the Skewers also made a part of the shew,
  With which they were trussed for the spit.

The Cook in triumph bore that Spit
As high as he was able;
And the Dish was display'd wherein they were laid
When they had been served at table.

With eager faith the crowd prest round;
There was a scramble of women and men
For who should dip a finger-tip
In the blessed Gravy then.

Next went the Alcayde, beating his breast,
Crying aloud like a man distrest,
And amazed at the loss of his dinner,
' " Santiago! Santiago!
Have mercy on me a sinner!"

And lifting oftentimes his hands
Towards the Cock and Hen,
" Orate pro nobis !" devoutly he cried,

And as devoutly the people replied,
Whenever he said it, " Amen!"

The Father and Mother were last in the train ;
Rejoicingly they came,
And extolled, with tears of gratitude,
Santiago's glorious name.

So, with all honours that might be,
They gently unhang'd Pierre ;
No hurt or harm had he sustained,
But, to make the wonder clear,
A deep black halter-mark remained
Just under his left ear.

PART IV.

AND now, my little listening dears,
With open mouths and open ears,
Like a rhymer whose only art is
That of telling a plain unvarnish'd tale,
To let you know, I must not fail,
What became of all the parties.

Pierre went on to Compostella
To finish his pilgrimage:
His Parents went back with him joyfully;
After which they returned to their own country;
And there, I believe, that all the three
Lived to a good old age.

For the gallows on which Pierre
So happily had swung,

It was resolved that never more
On it should man be hung.

To the Church it was transplanted,
    As ancient books declare;
And the people in commotion,
    With an uproar of devotion,
Set it up for a relic there.

What became of the halter I know not,
    Because the old books show not;
But we may suppose and hope,
That the City presented Pierre
    With that interesting rope.

For in his family, and this
    The Corporation knew,
It rightly would be valued more
    Than any *cordon bleu.*

The Innkeeper's wicked daughter
Confess'd what she had done,
So they put her in a Convent,
And she was made a Nun.

The Alcayde had been so frighten'd,
That he never ate fowls again;
And he always pull'd off his hat
When he saw a Cock and Hen.
Wherever he sat at table
Not an egg might there be placed:
And he never even muster'd courage for a custard,
Tho' garlic tempted him to taste
Of an omelet now and then.

But always after such a transgression
He hasten'd away to make confession;
And not till he had confess'd,
And the Priest had absolved him, did he feel
His conscience and stomach at rest.

The twice-born Birds to the Pilgrim's Church,
     As by miracle consecrated,
Were given; and there unto the Saint
     They were publicly dedicated.

At their dedication the Corporation
     A fund for their keep supplied.
And, after following the Saint and his banners,
This Cock and Hen were so changed in their manners,
     That the Priests were edified.

Gentle as any turtle dove,
Saint Cock became all meekness and love:
     Most dutiful of wives,
Saint Hen she never peck'd again,
     So they led happy lives.

The ways of ordinary fowls
You must know they had clean forsaken.

N

And if every cock and hen in Spain
Had their example taken,
Why then...the Spaniards would have had
No eggs to eat with bacon.

These blessed Fowls, at seven years end,
In the odour of sanctity died:
They were carefully pluck'd, and then
They were buried, side by side.

And lest the fact should be forgotten,
(Which would have been a pity,)
'Twas decreed, in honour of their worth,
That a Cock and Hen should be borne thenceforth
In the arms of that ancient City.

Two eggs Saint Hen had laid, no more ;
The chicken were her delight;
A Cock and Hen they proved,
And both, like their parents, were virtuous and white

The last act of the holy Hen
Was to rear this precious brood; and, when
Saint Cock and she were dead,
This couple, as the lawful heirs,
Succeeded in their stead.

They also lived seven years,
And they laid eggs but two;
From which two milk-white chicken
To Cock and Henhood grew:
And always their posterity
The self-same course pursue.

Not one of these eggs ever addled,
(With wonder be it spoken!)
Not one of them ever was lost,
Not one of them ever was broken.

Sacred they are; neither magpie, nor rat,

Snake, weasel, nor martin approaching them:
And woe to the irreverent wretch
Who should even dream of poaching them!

Thus then is this great miracle
Continued to this day;
And to their Church all Pilgrims go,
When they are on the way;
And some of the feathers are given them;
For which they always pay.

No price is set upon them,
And this leaves all persons at ease;
The Poor give as much as they can,
The Rich as much as they please.

But that the more they give the better,
Is very well understood;

Seeing whatever is thus disposed of,
    Is for their own souls' good;

For Santiago will always
    Befriend his true believers;
And the money is for him, the Priests
    Being only his receivers.

To make the miracle the more,
Of these feathers there is always store,
    And all are genuine too;
All of the original Cock and Hen,
    Which the Priests will swear is true.

Thousands a thousand times told have bought them,
And if myriads and tens of myriads sought them,
    They would still find some to buy;
For however great were the demand,
    So great would be the supply.

And if any of you, my small friends,
Should visit those parts, I dare say
You will bring away some of the feathers,
And think of old Robin Gray.

NOTES

TO THE

PILGRIM TO COMPOSTELLA.

A ship of marble made.—p. 155.

The marble ship I have not found any where except in Geddes: who must have found it in some version of the legend which has not fallen into my hands. But that the ship was made of marble I believe to be quite as true as any other part of the legend of Santiago... Whether of marble or not, it was a miraculous ship which, without oars or sails, performed the voyage from Joppa to Iria Flava, now El Padron, in Galicia, in seven days.

Classical fables were still so passable when the Historia Compostelana was written, that the safe passage of this ship over the Syrtes, and between Scylla and Charybdis, is ascribed to the presiding hand of Providence.—*España Sagrada*, t. xx. p. 6.

...his headless corpse.—p. 155.

How the body came to leave its head behind is a circumstance which has not been accounted for: and yet it requires explanation, because we are assured that Santiago took particular care not to part with his head, when it was cut off.

" At the moment," says the Annalist of Galicia, " when the cruel executioner severed from its neck the

precious head of the sacred Apostle, the body miracu-
lously raised its hands and caught it, and in that posture
it continued till night. The astonished Jews attempted
to separate it, but in vain; for upon touching the venerable corpse their arms became cold, as if frozen, and
they remained without the use of them."—*Añales de
Galicia, por El Doctor D. Francisco Xavier Manuel
de la Huerta y Vega.*—Santiago, 1733.

" *Cortada la cabeza no dio en tierra,*
        Que por virtud de Dios, el con las manos,
    Antes que cayga al suelo a si la afierra,
        Que no pueden quitarsela tyranos."
Christoval de Mesa : *El Patron de España*, ff. 62.

Perhaps his companions dropt it on their way to the
coast, for the poet tells us they travelled in the dark, and
in a hurry :

" *Cubiertos de la noche con el manto*
        Sin que ningun contrario los impida,
    Mas presto que si fueran a galope,
        Llevan el cuerpo a la ciudad de Jope."
                                                    Ib. ff. 65.

But according to the *Historia Compostelana*, (España
Sagrada, t. xx. p. 6,) there is the testimony of Pope
St. Leo, that the original head came with the body.

And how, tho' then he had no head,
He afterwards had two.—p. 155.

This is a small allowance, and must be understood with reference to the two most authentic ones in that part of the world, .. that at Braga, and one of the two at Compostella.

It is a common thing for Saints to be polycephalous; and Santiago is almost as great a pluralist in heads as St. John the Baptist has been made by the dealers in relics. There are some half dozen heads, and almost as many whole bodies ascribed to him, .. all in good odour, all having worked miracles, and all, beyond a doubt, equally authentic.

And how he used to fight the Moors.—p. 156.

Most appropriately therefore, according to P. Sautel, was he called Boanerges.

" *Conspicitur medio cataphractus in aere ductor,*
Qui dedit in trepidam barbara castra fugam.
Tam cito tam validæ cur terga dedere phalanges?
Nimirum Tonitru Filius ista patrat."
                    Annus Sacer Poeticus, vol. ii. p. 32.

... " *siendo acá en España nuestro amparo y defensa en*

*las guerras, mereció con razon este nombre : pues mas
feroz que trueno ni rayo espantaba, confundia y desba-
rataba los grandes exercitos de los Moros."*—Morales,
Coronica Gen. de España, l. ix. c. vii. § 4.

" *Vitoria Espana, vitoria,
　　que tienes en tu defensa,
　　uno de los Doze Pares ;
　　mas no de nacion Francesa.
　　Hijo es tuyo, y tantos mata,
　　que parece que su fuerza
　　excede a la de la muerte
　　quando mas furiosa y presta.*"
Ledesma, *Conceptos Espirituales*, p. 242.

The Spanish Clergy had a powerful motive for propa-
gating these fables; their *Privilegio de los votos* being
one of the most gainful, as well as most impudent
forgeries, that ever was committed.

" The two sons of Zebedee manifested," says Morales,
" their courage and great heart, and the faith which was
strengthening in them, by their eagerness to revenge
the injury done to their kinsman and master when the
Samaritans would not receive him into their city. Then
Santiago and St. John distinguished themselves from the
other Apostles, by coming forward, and saying to our
Saviour, ' Lord, wilt thou that we command fire to come
down from Heaven and consume them ?' It seems as

if (according to the Castilian proverb concerning kins-
men) their blood boiled in them to kill and to destroy,
because of the part which they had in his. But be not
in such haste, O glorious Apostle Santiago, to shed the
blood of others for Christ your cousin-german! It will
not be long before you will give it to him, and for him
will give all your own. Let him first shed his for you,
that, when yours shall be mingled with it by another new
tie of spiritual relationship, and by a new friendship in
martyrdom, it shall be more esteemed by him, and held
in great account. Let the debt be well made out, that
the payment may be the more due. Let the benefit be
compleated, that you may make the recompense under
greater obligation, and with more will. Then will it be
worth more, and manifest more gratitude. Learn meantime from your Master, that love is not shown in killing
and destroying the souls of others, for the beloved, but
in mortifying and offering your own to death. This,
which is the height and perfection of love, your Master
will teach you, and thenceforth you will not content
yourself with anything less. And if you are desirous,
for Christ's sake, to smite and slay his enemies, have
patience awhile, fierce Saint! (*Santo feroz.*) There
will come a time when you shall wage war for your
Master, sword in hand, and in your person shall slaughter
myriads and myriads of Moors, his wicked enemies!"—
Coronica General de España, l. ix. c. vii. § 8.

An old hymn, which was formerly used in the service
of his day, likens this Apostle to... a Lion's whelp!

> *Electus hic Apostolus,*
> *Decorus et amabilis,*
> *Velut Leonis catulus*
> *Vicit bella certaminis."*
>> Divi Tutelares, 229.

" Thirty-eight visible appearances," says the Padre
Maestro Fray Felipe de la Gandara, Chronicler General
of the Kingdom of Galicia, .. " thirty-eight visible
appearances, in as many different battles, aiding and
favouring the Spaniards, are recounted by the very
learned Don Miguel Erce Gimenez in his most erudite
and laborious work upon the Preaching of Santiago in
Spain; from which work the *illustrissimous* Doctor Don
Antonio Calderon has collected them in his book upon
the Excellencies of this Apostle. And I hold it for certain that his appearances have been many more; and
that in every victory, which the Spaniards have achieved
over their enemies, this their Great Captain has been
present with his favour and intercession."—*Armas i Triunfos del Reino de Galicia*, p. 648.

The Chronista General proceeds to say that Galicia
may be especially proud of its part in all these victories,
the Saint having publicly prided himself upon his connection with that kingdom; for being asked in battle

once, who and what he was, (being a stranger,) he
replied, " I am a Soldier, a Kinsman of the Eternal
King, a Citizen and Inhabitant of Compostella, and my
name is James." For this fact the Chronicler assures us
that a book of manuscript sermons, preached in Paris
three centuries before his time by a Franciscan Friar,
is sufficient authority : " *es valiente autoridad!*"—Armas
¡ Triunfos del Reino de Galicia, p. 649.

... Still they worship him in Spain,
And believe in him with might and main.—p. 156.

... " *calamo describi vix potest, aut verbis exprimi,*
quanto in Jacobum Apostolum Hispani amore ferantur,
quam tenero pietatis sensu festos illius dies, et memoriam
celebrent ; quam se, suaque omnia, illius fidei et clientelæ
devoveant ; ipsius auspiciis bellicas expeditiones suscipere,
et conficere soliti, et Jacobi nomine quasi tesserâ se
milites illius esse profiteri.   Cum pugnam ineunt, ut sibi
animos faciant et hostibus terrorem incutiant, in primâ,
quæ vehementior esse solet, impressione, illam vocem in-
tonant, Sancte Jacobe, urge Hispania, *hoc est,* Santiago,
cierra Hespanha ; *militari se illi sacramento addicunt ;*
et illustrissimo Equitum Ordine Jacobi nomine instituto,
ejusque numini sacro, cujus Rex ipse Catholicus Magnus
Magister et Rector est : ejus se obsequiis dedicant et

*legibus adstringunt, ut nullius erga quenquam alium
Sanctum Patronum gentis clariora extent, quam Hispa-
nicæ erga Jacobum amoris et religionis indicia. Quàm
verò bene respondeat huic amori et pietati Apostolus
curâ, et solicitudine Patris et Patroni, ex rebus à suis
clientibus, ejus auxilio, præclarè gestis, satis constat, tum
in ipsa Hispania, tum in utráque, ad Orientem et Occi-
dentem Solem Indiá, Hispanorum et Lusitanorum armis
subactâ, et illorum operâ et industriá ubique locorum
propagatâ Christianâ religione.*"—P. Ant. Macedo. Divi
Tutelares Orbis Christiani, p. 228.

Santiago there they call him.—p. 156.

" The true name of this Saint," says Ambrosio de
Morales, " was Jacobo, (that is, according to the Spanish
form,) taken with little difference from that of the Patri-
arch Jacob. A greater is that which we Spaniards have
made, corrupting the word little by little, till it has
become the very different one which we now use. From
Santo Jacobo we shortened it, as we commonly do with
proper names, and said Santo Jaco. We clipt it again
after this abbreviation, and by taking away one letter,
and changing another, made it into Santiago. The
alteration did not stop here; but because Yago or Tiago
by itself did not sound distinctly and well, we began to

call it Diago, as may be seen in Spanish writings of two
or three hundred years old. At last, having past through
all these mutations, we rested with Diego for the ordinary name, reserving that of Santiago when we speak of
the Saint."—*Coronica General de España*, l. ix. c. vii.
§ 2.

Florez pursues the corruption further : " *nombrandole
por la voz latina* Jacobus Apostolus, *con abreviacion y
vulgaridad* Jacobo Apostolo, ò Giacomo Postolo, ò Jiac
Apostol."—*España Sagrada*, t. xix. p. 71.

It has not been explained how *Jack* in this country
was transferred from James to John.

The Prior Cayrasco de Figueroa assures us that
St. James was a gentleman, his father Zebedee being

" *Varon de ilustre sangre y Galileo,
Puesto que usava el arte piscatoria,
Que entonces no era illicito, ni feo,
Ni aora en muchas partes menos gloria,
La gente principal tener oficio,
O por su menester, o su exercicio.*"

Templo Militante, p. iii. p. 83.

Morales also takes some pains to establish this point.
Zebedee, he assures us, " *era hombre principal, señor de
un navio, con que seguia la pesca :*" and it is clear, he
says, " *como padre y hijos seguian este trato de la pes-
queria honradamente, mas como señores que como ofici-
ales !*"—Coronica Gen. de España, l. ix. c. vii. § 3.

o

They've an Inquisition to maul him.—p. 156.

Under the dominion of that atrocious Tribunal Ambrosio de Morales might truly say, " no one will dare deny that the body of the glorious Apostle is in the city which is named after him, and that it was brought thither, and afterwards discovered there by the great miracles,".. of which he proceeds to give an account. " People have been burnt for less,".. as a fellow at Leeds said the other day of a woman whom he suspected of bewitching him.

There is nothing of which the Spanish and Portugueze authors have boasted with greater complacency and pleasure than of the said inquisition. A notable example of this is afforded in the following passage from the *Templo Militante, Flos Santorum, y Triumphos de sus Virtudes,* by D. Bartolome Cayrasco de Figueroa, Prior and Canon of the Cathedral Church of Grand Canary. (Lisbon, 1613.)

> " —————— *gloriosa España,*
> *Aunque de mucho puedes gloriarte,*
> *No está en esso el valor que te acompaña,*
> *Sino en tener la Fè por estandarte :*
> *Por esta la provincia mas estraña,*
> *Y todo el orbe teme de enojarte ;*
> *Por esta de tu nombre tiembla el mundo*
> *Y el cavernoso Tartaro profundo.*

" *Agradecelo a Dios de cuya mano*
Procede toda gracia, toda gloria ;
Y despues del al Principe Christiano,
Philipo digno de immortal memoria :
Porque con su govierno soberano,
Con su justicia, y su piedad notoria,
Estas assegurada, y defendida,
De todos los peligros desta vida.

" *Este gran Rey decora tu terreno*
Con veynte y dos insignes fortalezas,
Cuyos fuertes Alcaydes ponen freno
A todas las tartaricas bravezas :
Y con temor del malo, honor del bueno,
Castigan las malicias, y simplezas
De hereticas palabras y opiniones,
Que son las veynte y dos Inquisiciones.

" *De la Imperial Toledo es la primera ;*
De la Real Sevilla la segunda,
De Cordova la ilustre la tercera,
La quarta de Granqda la fecunda :
Tambien en Calahorra la vandera
De la sagrada Inquisicion se funda,
Y Margaritas son desta corona,
Zaragoza, Valencia, Barcelona.

" *Tambien Valladolid aventajada :*
o 2

Despues del gran incendio, en edificio ;
Cuenca, Murcia, Llerena celebrada
En mucha antiguedad del Santo Oficio:
En Galicia assi mismo esta fundada
Torre deste santissimo exercicio,
En Evora, en Coimbra, en Ulisipo,
Que ya la Lusitania es de Philipo.

" *Tambien Sicilia en esta viva peña*
De la importante Inquisicion estriva ;
Y Gran Canaria en publica reseña
Los adversarios de la Fe derriba :
Las islas de Mallorca y de Cerdeña,
Y el gran Reyno que fue de Atabalipa,
Y la postrera desta heroyca suma
Es la ciudad que fue de Motezuma.

" *Sobre estas fortalezas de importancia*
Esta la general torre suprema,
Fundada sobre altissima constancia,
Cubierta de Catolica diadema :
De cuya soberana vigilancia,
Resplendeciente luz, virtud estrema,
Procede a las demas, la fuerza, el brio,
El Christiano valor, el poderio.

" *Estes pues son los celebres Castillos,*
De la Fé verdaderos defensores,

Que con habitos roxos y amarillos,
Castigan los heretycos errores :
Y a los pechos Catolicos sensillos,
De la verdad Christiana zeladores,
Les dan el justo premio, honor devido,
De la virtud heroyca merecido."

The Poet proceeds to eulogize Santiago as having
been the founder in Spain of that faith for the defence
and promotion of which these two-and-twenty Castles
were erected.

" *Pues si en el mundo es digno de memoria*
El fundador de una ciudad terrena ;
Y luego es celebrada en larga historia
El inventor de alguna cosa buena,
Que premio le daras? que honor? que gloria?
Felice España, de virtudes llena,
Al que fue de la Fé que aqui refiero,
En tus Provincias fundador primero?

" *Razon será, que su memoria sea*
En todo tu distrito eternizada,
Y que en aqueste Santoral se lea
(Aunque con debil pluma) celebrada :
Pues alto España, porque el mundo vea
Que puedes en la Fé mas que en la espada,
Da me atentos oydos entretanto
Que de tu Cavallero ilustre canto.

" *Oygaume los magnanimos guerreros*
Que ponen freno al barbaro despecho,
Y en especial aquellos Cavalleros
Que adornan de su insinia roxa el pecho :
Veran que los blasones verdaderos
Se alcanzan, imitando en dicho y hecho
Al Español caudillo Santiago
Gran zelador del Agareno estrago."

P. iii. p. 81.

———

At Compostella in his Church
His body and one head
Have been, for some eight hundred years,
By Pilgrims visited.—p. 156.

" ——— *a visitar el cuerpo santo*
Todo fiel Christiano la via toma :
Adonde viene peregrino tanto
Como a Jerusalem, y como a Roma,
Que a el de tierra y mar por los caminos
Vienen de todo el mundo peregrinos.

" *Varia gente fiel, pueblo devoto,*
El Santuario celebre frequenta,
Acude el casi naufrago piloto,
Libre de la maritima tormenta :

Que del mar combatido hizo voto,
Teniendo de salvar el alma cuenta,
Que de la tempestad casi sin habla,
Con la vida salio sobre una tabla.

" *El coxo del lugar propio se alexa*
De una azemila o carro hecho carga,
Y representa su piadosa quexa,
De aquella enfermedad prolixa y larga :
Buelve en sus pies, y las muletas dexa,
Y de alguna piadosa obra se encarga,
Gratificando con palabras santas,
Poder bolver sobre sus propias plantas.

" *El que ya tuvo vista, y no tiene ojos,*
Al Templo viene del Apostol Diego,
Haze oracion, y postrase de hinojos,
Buelve con luz, aviendo entrado ciego :
Y ojos de cera dexa por despojos,
De que alcancó salud su humilde ruego,
Y en recompensa de la nueva vista,
Es del raro milagro coronista.

" *El que hablar no puede, aunque con lengua*
Que subito accidente hizo mudo,
Pide remedio de su falta y mengua,
Con un sonido balbuciente y rudo :

Su devocion humilde su mal mengua,
Y pudiendo dezir lo que no pudo,
Con nueva voz, y con palabras claras,
Haze gracias por dadivas tan raras.

" *Si aqueste viene de sus miembros manco,*
   Y aquel sordo del todo, otro contrecho,
   Con todos el Apostol es tan franco,
   Con su medio con Dios es de provecho :
   Cada qual con alegre habito blanco,
   Buelve de su demanda satisfecho,
   Dando buelta a su tierra los dolientes,
   Sanos de enfermedades diferentes.

" *A quien de prision saca, ó cautiverio,*
   Remedia enfermos, muertos resucita,
   Da a los desconsolados refrigerio,
   Y diferentes aflicciones quita :
   Sobre toda dolencia tiene imperio,
   La milagrosa fabrica bendita,
   Libra de muerte en agua, en hierro, en fuego,
   El cuerpo santo del Apostol Diego.

" *Da toda alma fiel gracias al cielo,*
   Que perdonado al pecador què yerra,
   Para remedio suyo, y su consuelo,
   Tal bien el Reyno de Galizia encierra :

*Para que venga desde todo el suelo
A las postreras partes de la tierra,
Todo fiel Catolico Christiano,
A implorar el auxilio soberano."*
Cristoval de Mesa, El Patron de España, ff. lxxii. p. 3.

The high altar at Compostella is, as all the altars formerly were in Galicia and Asturias, not close to the
wall, but a little detached from it. It is ten feet in
length, and very wide, with a splendid frontispiece of
silver. The altar itself is hollow, and at the Gospel end
there is a small door, never opened except to royal
visitors, and when a new Archbishop first comes to take
possession. It was opened for Ambrosio de Morales,
because he was commissioned to inspect the churches:
nothing, however, was to be seen within, except two
large flat stones, which formed the floor, and at the end
of them a hole about the size of an orange, but filled
with mortar. Below is the vault in which the body of
Santiago is said to be deposited in the marble coffin
wherein it was found. The vault extends under the
altar and its steps, and some way back under the Capella
Mayor: it is in fact a part of the Crypt walled off with
a thick wall, *para dexar cerrado del todo el santo
cuerpo.*

The Saint, whose real presence is thus carefully con-
cealed, receives his pilgrims in effigy. The image is a
half figure of stone, a little less than life, gilt and painted,

holding in one hand a book, and as if giving a blessing
with the other. *Esta en cabello,* without either crown
or glory on the head, but a large silver crown is
suspended immediately above, almost so as to touch the
head; and the last ceremony which a pilgrim performs
is to ascend to the image, which is over the altar, by a
stair-case from the Epistle side, kiss it reverently on the
head, embrace it, and place this crown upon it, and then
go down on the Gospel side.—*Viage de Morales,* t. xx.
p. 154.

> " *Ingens sub. templo fornix, et claustra per umbras*
> *Magna jacent, cæcæque domus, queis magna Jacobi*
> *Ossa sepulchrali fama est in sede latere.*
> *Nulli fas hominum sacratum insistere limen ;*
> *Est vidisse nefas, nec eundi pervius usus :*
> *E longè veniam exorant atque oscula figunt*
> *Liminibus, redeuntque domos ; variasque galeris*
> *Jacobi effigies addunt, humcrosque bacillis*
> *Circundant, conchisque super fulgentibus ornant.*"
>
> Paciecis, lib. vii. p. 117.

The sepulchre was thus closed by the first Archbishop
D. Diego Gelmirez, " *que ya de ninguna manera se*
puede ver, ni entenderse como está. Y esto hizo con
prudentissimo consejo aquel gran Principe y valeroso
Perlado, y con reverencia devota, porque cada uno no
quisiese ver y tratar aquel precioso relicario comunmente,
y sin el debido respete ; que se pierde sin duda quando los

*cuerpos santos y sus sepulturas pueden ser vistas vulgar-
mente de todos.*"—Morales, l. ix. c. vii. § 67.

A print of the sepulchre, from an illuminated drawing
in the manuscript of the *Historia Compostelana*, is given
in the 20th volume of the *España Sagrada*. And in
that history (pp. 50, 51) is the following characteristic
account of the enlargement of the altar by D. Diego
Gelmirez.

" Among the other worthinesses, with the which the
aforesaid Bishop in no inactive solicitude hastened to
decorate his Church, we have been careful to defend
from the death of oblivion whatsoever his restauratory
hand did to the altar of the said Church. But, lest in
bringing forward all singular circumstances we should
wander into devious ways, we will direct our intention
to the straight path, and commit to succeeding remembrance so far as our possibility may reveal those things
which we beheld with our own eyes. For of how small
dimensions the altar of Santiago ·formerly was, lest we
should be supposed to diminish it in our relation, may
better be collected from the measure of the altarlet itself.
But as religion increased in the knowledge of the
Christian faith, that another altarlet, a little larger than
the other, was placed over it by those who were zealous
for their holy faith, our ancient fathers have declared
unto us as well by faithful words, as by the assured testimony of writings. But the aforesaid Bishop being
vehemently desirous of increasing the beauty of his

Church, and seeing that this little altar, though thus enlarged, was altogether unworthy of so great an Apostle,
thought it worthy of pious consideration to aggrandize
the Apostolical altar.   Wherefore, being confirmed
thereunto by the prudent counsel of religious men,
although the Canons stoutly resisted him in this matter,
he declared his determination to demolish the habitacle
which was made in the likeness of the sepulchre below,
in which sepulchre we learn, without all doubt, that the
remains of the most holy Apostle are inclosed.   They
indeed repeatedly asserted that a work which, rude and
deformed as it was, was nevertheless edified in honour
to the remains of such holy personages, ought by no
means to be destroyed, lest they themselves or their lord
should be stricken with lightning from heaven, and suffer
the immediate punishment of such audacity.   But he,
like a strenuous soldier, protected with the impenetrable
shield of a good resolution, forasmuch as, with the eye
of his penetration, he perceived that they regarded
external things more than inner ones, trampled upon
their fears with the foot of his right intention, and levelled
to the ground their habitacle, and enlarged the altar,
which had originally been so small a one, now for the
third time, with marble placed over and about it on all
sides, making it as it ought to be.   Without delay also
he marvellously began a silver frontispiece for this egre-
gious and excellent work, and more marvellously compleated it."

There used to be interpreters at Compostella for all languages; *lenguageros* they were called. They had a silver wand, with a hand and finger pointed at the top, to show the relics with. Among those relics is the head of St. James the less; a grinder, in a splendid gold reliquary, of one St. James, it has not been determined which; one of St. Christopher's arms, of modest dimensions; and seven heads of the Eleven Thousand Virgins. These are from the list which Morales gives: but that good and learned man, who often swallowed the bull and stuck at the tail, omits some more curious ones, which are noticed in an authentic inventory. (España Sagrada, t. xix. p. 344.) Among these are part of our Lord's raiment, of the earth on which he stood, of the bread which he brake, of his blood, and of the Virgin's milk.

A late editor of Old Fortunatus is reminded in one of his notes of Martinus Scriblerus, by a passage in the play, which, as he should have seen, is evidently allusive to such relics as those at Compostella.

———— " there can I show thee
The ball of gold that set all Troy on fire:
There shalt thou see the scarf of Cupid's mother,
Snatch'd from the soft moist ivory of her arm
To wrap about Adonis' wounded thigh:
There shalt thou see a wheel of Titan's car,
Which dropp'd from Heaven when Phaeton fir'd the
world.

I'll give thee...the fan of Proserpine,
Which, in reward for a sweet Thracian song,
The black-browed Empress threw to Orpheus,
Being come to fetch Eurydice from hell."

...All who in their mortal stage
Did not perform this pilgrimage,
Must make it when they were dead.—p. 157.

" *Huc Lysiæ properant urbes, huc gentes Iberæ*
Turbæ adeunt, Gallique omnes, et Flandria cantu
Insignis, populique Itali, Rhenusque bicornis
Confluit, et donis altaria sacra frequentant;
Namque ferunt vivi qui non hæc templa patentes
Invisunt, post fata illuc, et funeris umbras
Venturos, munusque istud præstare beatis
Lacte viam stellisque albam, quæ nocte serenâ
Fulgurat, et longo designat tramite cælum."
        P. Bartholome Pereira, *Paciecidos*, lib. vii. p. 117.

Fray Luys de Escobar has this among the five hundred proverbs of his Litany,

        ...*el camino a la muerte*
        es como el de Santiago.
                Las quatrocientas, &c. ff. 140.

it seems to allude to this superstition, meaning, that it
is a journey which all must take. The particular part

of the pilgrimage, which must be performed either in ghost or in person, is that of crawling through a hole in the rock at El Padron, which the Apostle is said to have made with his staff.   In allusion to this part of the pilgrimage, which is not deemed so indispensable at Compostella as at Padron, they have this proverb, *Quien va á Santiago, y non va á Padron, ó faz Romeria ó non.* The pilgrim, indeed, must be incurious who would not extend his journey thither; a copious fountain, of the coldest and finest water which Morales tasted in Galicia, rises under the high altar, but on the outside of the church; the pilgrims drink of it, and wash in its waters, as the Apostle is said to have done : they ascend the step in the rock upon their knees, and finally perform the passage which must be made by all : " *y cierto, considerado el sitio, y la hermosa vista que de alli hay á la ciudad, que estaba abaxo en lo llano, y á toda la ancha hoya llena de grandes arboledas y frescuras de mas de dos leguas en largo, lugar es aparejado para mucha contemplacion.*"—Viage de Morales, p. 174.

One of Pantagruel's *Questions Encyclopédiques* is, " *Utrum le noir Scorpion pourroit souffrir solution de continuité en sa substance, et par l'effusion de son sang obscurcir et embrunir la voye lactée, au grand interest et dommage des Lifrelofres Jacobipetes.*"—Rabelais, t. ii. p. 417.

The scallop-shell.—p. 159.

" The escallops, being denominated by ancient authors
the *Shells of Gales,* or *Galicia,* plainly apply to this pilgrimage in particular."—*Fosbrooke, British Monachism,*
p. 423.

Fuller is therefore mistaken when speaking of the
Dacres family, (Church Hist. cent. xii. p. 42,) who gave
their arms *gules,* three scallop-shells argent, he says,
" which scallop-shells, (I mean the nethermost of them,
because most concave and capacious,) smooth within,
and artificially plated without, was oft times cup and
dish to the pilgrims in Palestine, and thereupon their
arms often charged therewith."

That the scallop belonged exclusively to the Compostella pilgrim is certain, as the following miracle may
show.

" The ship, in which the body of the Apostle was
embarked, passed swiftly by a village in Portugal called
Bouzas, wherein there dwelt a noble and powerful lord,
who on that day married one of his daughters to the son
of another person as considerable as himself, lord of the
land of Amaya. The nuptials were celebrated in the
village of Bouzas, and many noble knights of that pro-
vince came to the solemnity. One of their sports was
that of throwing the cane, and in this the bridegroom
chose to bear a part, commanding a troop, that he might
display his dexterity. The place for the sport was on

the coast of the ocean, and the bridegroom's horse, becoming ungovernable, plunged into the sea, and sunk
under the immensity of its waters, and, at the moment
when the ship was passing by, rose again close beside it.
There were several miracles in this case. The first was,
that the sea bore upon its waves the horse and horse-
man, as if it had been firm land, after not having
drowned them when they were so long a time under
water. The second was, that the wind, which was
driving the ship in full speed to its port, suddenly fell,
and left it motionless; the third, and most remarkable,
was, that both the garments of the knight, and the trappings of the horse, came out of the sea covered with
scallop-shells.

" The knight, astonished at such an unexpected
adventure, and seeing the disciples of the Apostle, who
with equal astonishment were looking at him from the
ship, asked them what it was that had brought him
where he found himself. To which the disciples, being
inspired by heaven, replied, ' that certes Christ, through
the merit of a certain servant of his, whose body they
were transporting in that ship, had chosen to manifest
his power upon him, for his good, by means of this
miracle.' The knight then humbly requested them to
tell him who Christ was, and who was that Servant of
his of whom they spake, and what was the good which
he was to derive. The disciples then briefly catechised
him; and the knight, having thus been instructed, said

P

to them, ' Friends and Sirs, you, who have served Christ
and his holy Apostle, which I as yet have not done, ask
of him to show you for what purpose he has put these
scallop-shells upon me, because so strange a marvel
cannot have been wrought without some great mystery.'
With that the disciples made their prayer accordingly,
and, when they had prayed, they heard a voice from
Heaven, which said thus unto the knight, ' Our Lord
Christ has thought good to show by this act all persons
present and to come, who may choose to love and serve
this his servant, and who shall go to visit him where he
shall be interred, that they take with them from thence
other such scallop-shells as these with which thou art
covered, as a seal of privilege, confirming that they are
his, and will be so from that time forward : and he pro-
mises that afterwards, in the Day of the Last Judgement,
they shall be recognised of God for his ; and that, because
of the honours which they have done to this his servant
and friend, in going to visit him and to venerate him,
he will receive them into his glory and his Paradise.'

" When the knight heard these words, immediately
he made the disciples baptize him ; and while they were
so doing, he noticed, with devotion and attention, the
ceremonies of the sacred ministry, and when it was done,
he took his leave of them, commending himself to their
grace, and intreating of them that they would commend
him in their prayers to Christ and his Apostle Santiago.
At that instant the wind, which till then had been still,

struck the sails, and the ship began to cleave the wide
sea. The knight then directed his course toward the
shore, riding upon the water, in sight of the great multitude, which from the shore was watching him; and
when he reached the shore, and was surrounded by
them, he related to them what had happened. The
natives, astonished at the sight of such stupendous
miracles, were converted, and the knight, with his own
hand, baptized his bride."

The facts are thus related, to the letter, in the *Sanctoral
Portugues*, from whence the Breviaries of Alcobaça and
St. Cucufate copied it, and that of Oviedo in the Hymn
for the Apostle's Day,.. from which authorities the mo-
derns have taken it. The Genealogists say that the
Visyras of Portugal are descended from this knight,
because the scallop is called by that name in their
tongue, and that family bear it in their arms. The
Pimenteles make the same pretensions, and also bear
four scallops in their shield. The Ribadaneyras also
advance a similar claim, and they bear a cross with five
scallops.

"This is the origin of the shells with which the pilgrims,
who come to visit the body of our glorious Patron, adorn
themselves, the custom having, without doubt, been preserved by tradition from that time. The circumstances
are confirmed by pictures representing it, which from
ancient times have been preserved in various cities. In
the Church of St. Maria de Aracoeli at Rome, on the

Gospel side, there is a spacious chapel, dedicated to our
glorious Patron; it was painted in the year 1441, and
in one compartment this adventure is represented: there
is the ship, having the body of the Apostle on the poop,
and the seven Disciples on board: close to the ship,
upon the sea, is a Knight upon a black horse, with a red
saddle and trappings, both covered with scallop-shells.
The same story is painted in the parish church of Santiago at Madrid: and it is related in a very ancient
manuscript, which is preserved in the library of the
Monastery of St. Juan de los Reyes, at Toledo. In the
Ancient Breviary of the Holy Church of Oviedo, mention
is made of this prodigy in these verses, upon the vesper
of the glorious Saint.

> ‘ Cunctis mare cernentibus,
>   Sed a profundo ducitur,
>   Natus Regis submergitur
>   Totus plenus conchilibus.’

Finally, the fact is authenticated by their Holinesses
Alexander III., Gregory IX., and Clement V., who in
their Bulls grant a faculty to the Archbishop of Compostella, that they may excommunicate those who sell these
shells to pilgrims anywhere except in the city of Santiago, and they assign this reason, because the shells are
the badge of the Apostle Santiago. And thus in the
Church of St. Clement at Rome, which is enriched with
the body of St. Clement, Pope and Martyr, is a picture of

the Apostle Santiago, apparently more than five hundred years old, which is adorned with scallop-shells on the garment and hat, as his proper badge."—*Añales de Galicia*, vol. i. pp. 95, 96.

Gwillim, in his account of this bearing, says nothing of its origin. But he says " the Escallop (according to Diascorides) is engendered of the Dew and Air, and hath no blood at all in itself, notwithstanding in man's body of any other food it turneth soonest into blood. The eating of this fish raw is said to cure a surfeit. Such (he adds) is the beautiful shape that nature hath bestowed upon this shell, as that the Collar of the Order of St. Michel in France, in the first institution thereof, was richly garnished with certain pieces of gold artificially wrought, as near as the artificer could by imitation express the stamp of nature."—*Display of Heraldry*, p. 171. (first edit.)

One of the three manners, in which Santiago is commonly represented, is in the costume of a Compostellan pilgrim, with a scallop-shell in his hat. All three are described in a book, as rare of occurrence as curious in its subject, thus entitled, Pictor Christianus Eruditus: *Sive, De Erroribus, qui passim admittuntur circa pingendas atque effingendas Sacras Imagines. Libri Octo cum Appendice. Opus Sacræ Scripturæ, atque Ecclesiasticæ Historiæ studiosis non inutile. Authore R. P. M. Fr. Joanne Interian de Ayala, Sacri, Regii, ac Militaris Ordinis Beatæ Mariæ de Mercede Redemp-*

tionis Captivorum, Salmanticensis Academiæ Doctore
Theológo, atque ibidem Sanctæ Theologiæ cum sacrarum
Linguarum interpretatione Professore jam pridem eme-
rito. *Anno D.* 1730, MATRITI: *Ex Typographia*
Conventus præfati Ordinis. fol.

One of the Censors of this book says, *prodit in lucem*
Pictor Christianus *eruditissimi pectoris eruditissimus*
fœtus, obstetricante N. RR. P. M. Fr. Josepho Campa-
zano de la Vega. The work was published by the
Master's direction at the cost of the Order; the Master
dedicated it to N. Señora de las Mercedes as *elaboratum,*
excultumque quantum potuit, by her assistance; and
there is a *censura* prefixed by Ferreras the Historian,
speaking forcibly of the importance of the undertaking,
and of the great ability with which it is executed.

Instead of perceiving that Santiago is represented in
the costume of his own pilgrims, this author supposed
that the Saint is so attired because he had travelled over
Spain! The whole passage is curious for its grave and
cool credulity. " *Sanctus Jacobus Zebedei filius, His-*
paniæ primarius (quidquid alii commenti sint) Patronus
atque Apostolus, bifariam sæpius a Pictoribus describitur.
Pingitur enim peregrini habitu, oblongo innixus baculo,
ex quo etiam bursa pendeat, et circa humeros amiculo,
quod Hispani Esclavinam *vocant; insuper et cum galero*
satis amplo, quem tamen ornant conchæ, quæ circa littus
maris passim se offerunt: Totum id ex eo arbitror pro-
ficisci, quod Hispaniam celerrimè, et ut decebat Tonitru

*filium, peragraverat : ubi postmodum corpus ejus è Hie-
rosolymis translatum condigno honore colitur. Sed ab
aliis etiam cum gladio pingitur, cumque libro aperto,*
' *Quæ pictura (inquit frequens nobis author) etsi rarior
sit, priori tamen est præferenda, quod ex Sacrá Scripturà
desumpta sit, et martyrium ejus explicat. Quod ita
habetur, Occidit autem Jacobum fratrem Joannis gladio.*
*Sæpè etiam pingitur equo insistens, armatusque gladio,
acies Maurorum impigrè perrumpens, eosque ad interne-
cionem usque cædens. Quod non exiguá cum Hispani
nominis gloriá rectè fit ; cùm sæpè visus sit pro Hispanis
in aëre pugnans ; de cujus rei fide dubium esse non potest iis qui interfuerunt ejus Ecclesiastico officio, ubi illud
metricè habetur*

> *Tu bello cùm nos cingerent,*
> *Et visus ipso in prælio,*
> *Equoque et ense acerrimus*
> *Mauros furentes sternere.*

Atque idem alibi solutá oratione describitur illis verbis :†
' *Ipse etiam gloriosus Apostolus in difficillimis præliis
palàm se conspiciendum præbens, Hispanos adversus Infi-
deles pugnantes mirificè juvit.' "*—Lib. vii. c. ii. pp. 320,
321.

* Molan. lib. iii. c. 26.
† In festo Translat. ejusdem. 30 Dec.

> ... *The Staff was bored and drilled for those*
> *Who on a flute could play.*—p. 159.

Sir John Hawkins says, " that the pilgrims to
St. James of Compostella excavated a staff, or walking
stick, into a musical instrument for recreation on their
journey."—*History of Music*, vol. iv. p. 139, quoted in
Fosbrooke's British Monachism, p. 469. Mr. Fosbrooke
thinks that " this ascription of the invention of the
Bourdon to these pilgrims in particular is very question-
able." Sir John probably supposed with Richelet that
the *Bourdon* was peculiar to these pilgrims, and therefore that they had invented it.

Mr. Fosbrooke more than doubts the Etymon from a
musical use. " The barbarous Greek Βαρδωνα," he observes, " signified a beast of burden, and the *Bourdon*
was a staff of support. But the various meanings of the
word, as given by Cotgrave, make out its history satis-
factory. *Bourdon*, a drone, or dorre-bee, (Richelet says
grosse mouche, ennemie des abeilles,) also the humming
or buzzing of bees; also the drone of a bagpipe; also a
pilgrim's staff; also a walking-staff, having a sword, &c.
within it.

" It was doubtless applied to the use of pitching the
note, or accompanying the songs which pilgrims used to
recreate themselves on their journeys, and supposed by
Menestrier to be hymns and canticles."—*Fosbrooke*,
p. 422.

In Germany " walking-sticks that serve as tubes for
pipes, with a compressing pump at one end to make a
fire, and a machine at the other for impaling insects
without destroying their beauty, are common." (*Hodg-
kin's Travels*, vol. ii. p. 135.) I have seen a telescope
and a barometer in a walking-stick, if that name may be
applied to a staff of copper.

The twice-born Cock and Hen.—p. 171.

There is another story of a bird among the miracles
of Santiago; the poor subject of the miracle was not so
fortunate as the Cock and Hen of the Alcayde : but the
story is true. It occurred in Italy; and the Spanish
fable is not more characteristic of the fraudulent prac-
tices carried on in the Romish Church, than the Italian
story is of the pitiable superstition which such frauds
fostered, and which was, and is to this day, encouraged
by the dignitaries of that church.

At the request of St. Atto, Bishop of Pistoja, the Pistojans say that some relics, taken from Santiago's most
precious head, were given to their church by the Archbishop of Compostella, Diego Gelmirez, a person well
known in Spanish history. " *Nullus umquam mortalium
hoc donum impetrare posset,*" he affirmed when he made

the gift, and the historian of the translator adds, " *quod
verè à Domino factum credimus et non dubitamus, sicut
manifestis et apertis indiciis manifestè et apertè miracula,
declarabunt.*" There is a good collection of these
miracles, but this of the Bird is the most remarkable.

" In those days," says the writer, " another miracle,
as pious as it is glorious, was wrought by the Lord, in
the which he who worthily perpends it will perceive
what may pertain to the edification of all those who visit
the shrine of Santiago, and of all faithful Christians.
About three weeks after the consecration of Santiago's
altar, a certain girl of the country near Pistoja was
plucking hemp in a garden; when she observed a pigeon
flying through the air, which came near her, and
alighted: upon which she put up a prayer to the Lord
Santiago, saying, ' O Lord Santiago, if the things which
are related of thee at Pistoja be true, and thou workest
miracles as the Pistojans affirm, give me this pigeon,
that it may come into my hands!' Forthwith the
pigeon rose from the spot where it had alighted, and, as
if it were a tame bird, came to her, and she took it in
her hands, and held it there as if it had been lifeless.
What then did the girl do? She carried it home,
showed it to her father, and to him and the rest of the
family related in what manner it had come to her hands.
Some of them said, ' let us kill it and eat it:' others said,
' do not hurt it, but let it go.' So the girl opened her
hand, to see what it would do. The pigeon, finding

itself at liberty, fled to the ground, and joined the poultry which were then picking up their food, nor did it afterwards go from the house, but remained in their company as if it belonged to them.

" All therefore regarding, with no common wonder, the remarkable tameness of this pigeon, which indeed was not a tame bird but a wild one, they went to a priest in the adjacent city, and acquainted him with the circumstances. The priest, giving good counsel to the girl and her father, as he was bound to do, said, ' we will go together to our Lord the Bishop on Sunday, and act as he may think proper to direct us in this matter.' Accordingly on the Sunday they went to Pistoja, and presented the pigeon to the Bishop, who with his Canons was then devoutly celebrating mass in honour of Santiago, upon the holy altar which had been consecrated to his honour. The Prelate, when he had listened to their story, took the bird, and placed it upon the wall of the chancel, which is round about the altar of Santiago, and there it remained three weeks, never departing from thence, excepting that sometimes, and that very seldom, it flew about the church, but always returned without delay to its own station, and there mildly, gently, harmlessly, and tamely continued; and rarely did it take food.

" But people from Lucca, and other strangers, plucked feathers from its neck, that they might carry them away for devotion, and moreover, that they might exhibit them to those who had not seen the bird itself. From

such injuries it never attempted to defend itself, though
its neck was skinned by this plucking, and this the
unthinking people continued to do, till at length the
pigeon paid the debt of nature. And it was no wonder
that it died; for how could any creature live that scarcely
ever ate or slept? People came thither night and day
from all parts, and one after another disturbed it; and
every night vigils were kept there, the clergy and the
people with loud voices singing praises to the Lord, and
many lights were continually burning there: how,
therefore, could it live, when it was never allowed to be
at rest? The clergy and people grieving at its death,
as indeed it was a thing to be lamented, took counsel,
and hung up the skin and feathers to be seen there by
all comers.

"In such and so great a matter what could be more
gratifying, what more convenient than this wonderful
sign which the Almighty was pleased to give us? There
is no need to relate anything more concerning the aforesaid pigeon; it was seen there openly and publicly by
all comers, so that not only the laity and clergy of that
city, but many religious people from other parts, abbots,
friars, clergy, and laity, are able to attest the truth. And
I also add this my testimony as a true and faithful witness, for I saw the pigeon myself for a whole week, and
actually touched it with my own hands."

There is a postscript to this story, as melancholy as the
tale itself. The sick, and the crippled, and the lame,

had been brought to this church, in expectation of
obtaining a miraculous cure by virtue of the new relics
which had arrived.   Among these was a poor woman
in the last stage of disease, who had been brought upon
her pallet into the church, and was laid in a corner, and
left there; nor was it observed that this poor creature
was *in articulo mortis*, till the pigeon flew to the place,
and alighted upon her, and so drew the attention of the
people in the church to the dying woman, *quam quidem,
prout credimus, nisi columba monstrasset, nemo mori-
entem vidisset.*   They removed her out of the church
just before she breathed her last,..and in consequence
of this miracle, as it was deemed, they gave her an
honourable funeral.——*Acta Sanctorum*, Jul. t. vi. p. 64.

————

*What became of the halter I know not,
Because the old books show not.*—p. 175.

" *Antiguedad sagrada, el que se arriedra
De te, sera su verso falto y manco.*"

So Christoval de Mesa observes when he proceeds to
relate how the rude stone, upon which the disciples of
Santiago laid his body when they landed with it in
Spain, formed itself into a sepulchre of white marble.——
El Patron de Espana. ff. 68.

FINIS.

WORKS

OF

ROBERT SOUTHEY, ESQ.

POET LAUREATE.

––––––––

I.

A SERIES of COLLOQUIES on the PROGRESS and
PROSPECTS of SOCIETY.
With Engravings. 2 vols. 8vo. *Nearly ready.*
" Respice, aspice, prospice."

II.

HISTORY of the LATE WAR in SPAIN and
PORTUGAL.
In 4 vols. 8vo. 2*l.* 2*s.*

III.

HISTORY of the LATE WAR in SPAIN and
PORTUGAL.
Vol. III. 4to. is in the press and will be published shortly.

IV.

The BOOK of the CHURCH.   Third Edition.
In 2 vols. 8vo. 1*l.* 4*s.*

V.

VINDICIÆ ECCLESIÆ ANGLICANÆ—The BOOK
of the CHURCH vindicated and amplified. 8vo.

VI.

The LIFE of GENERAL WOLFE.
Small 8vo. (For the FAMILY LIBRARY.)

VII.

LIFE of LORD NELSON.   New Edition.
2 vols. fc. 8vo. 10*s.*

BOOKS LATELY PUBLISHED

By MR. MURRAY.

1. The JOURNAL of a NATURALIST. Post 8vo. with Plates, 15s.

2. OXFORD and LOCKE. By LORD GREN-VILLE. 8vo. 4s.

3. Account of GUATEMALA. By G. A. THOMP-SON, Esq. Foolscap 8vo. 10s. 6d.

4. L'ORATORE ITALIANO. By the MARQUIS SPINETO. Third Edition. 12mo. 7s. 6d.

5. SECOND EXPEDITION into the INTERIOR of AFRICA. By the late CAPTAIN CLAPPERTON; with the Journal of LANDER, his faithful Servant. 4to. 2l. 2s.

6. MEMOIRS of the AFFAIRS of EUROPE. By LORD JOHN RUSSEL. Vol. II. 4to. 2l. 10s.

7. PROTESTANT SECURITIES suggested. By the Right Hon. R. WILMOT HORTON, M.P. 8vo. 6s.

8. SPEECH of M. T. SADLER, M.P. on the CATHOLIC QUESTION. Second Edition. 2s.

To be published in the course of the next six weeks.

1. A CHRONICLE of the CONQUEST of GRA-NADA. By the AUTHOR of the SKETCH BOOK. 2 vols. 8vo.

2. The LIFE and SERVICES of Captain PHILIP BEAVER, late of H. M. Ship Nisus. By CAPTAIN SMYTH, R.N. 8vo.

3. LIFE of NAPOLEON BUONAPARTE. 2 vols.

4. LIFE of BISHOP HEBER.

5. FOREST SCENES and INCIDENTS in the WILDS of NORTH AMERICA.

CPSIA information can be obtained at www.ICGtesting.com
Printed in the USA
BVOW06s1756140316

440283BV00022B/154/P